THE SPECTRUM COOK BOOK

©1992 by P.F. James and A.F. Bartlett

Library of Congress Cataloging in Publication data.

ISBN 1 873779 00 3

Published by Spectrum Publications of Geneva, Vienna and Munich.
Printed and bound by FotoDirect Ltd, Brighton

THE SPECTRUM COOK-BOOK

International Cuisine
at its simplest and best

SEVEN CULTURAL TRADITIONS

THE RESTAURATEUR: PHILIP F. JAMES
THE EDITOR: ALAN F. BARTLETT

THE SPECTRUM COOK BOOK

INDEX

INTRODUCTION

Despite Man's physical and mental development over the centuries, he remains dominated by the geography of the land in which he lives.

His rules of behaviour ultimately conform to his particular limitations of land and water which in turn determine his crops and therefore his pattern of living.

Man is truly what he eats, drinks and thinks. Thinking is a solitary activity, but we can all take pleasure in his many and varied tables around the world.

THE MAGIC OF THE SEVEN

Why seven cultural cuisines and why the omission of those whose delights are universally acknowledged and acclaimed?

In truth, the number is accidental. It could have been many more or even a few less. It so happens that those chosen are historically and culturally closely linked. Each includes in its recipes ingredients and preparations which are not widely used or applied by other cultures with which we are generally more familiar. We hope that this is but the first edition whose later publication will be expanded to include other culinary cultures.

But the unique advantage of this book is the opportunity for its reader to select and mix courses, not according to tradition, but in anticipation of contrasting yet complementary tastes. No single culture boasts a comprehensive excellence, but each offers outstanding experiences initially evolved through necessity and availability. Through centuries of trial and error the logical combinations of ingredients and taste have been refined and satisfied to produce an ultimate enjoyment.

Read the recipes. Let your mouth water as it will. Then translate that which your eye and mind has savoured into that which not only looks and smells good, but tastes great.

HOW TO USE THE SPECTRUM COOK-BOOK

Each Cuisine Section has a brief introduction to explain the background to the culinary approach adopted by those within a general geographic area or country or culture and why certain ingredients and wines might dominate that particular cuisine.

Where opportunity exists certain specialities are recommended.

Recipes are chosen for their originality of taste and simplicity of preparation.

Emphasis is given to fresh foods, freshly cooked.

It is no idle boast to suggest that the reader's taste buds will quickly blossom as the recipes are savoured.

This cook-book is not confined to any one race or creed. On the contrary it is designed for all who would like to sample the previously unknown delights of cuisines that represent the taste and experience of those who have long enjoyed that which they have guarded as their tradition and inheritance. At long last we can all exchange and share some of the true treasures of civilisation.

New and Additional Tastes

From time to time new Editions of the Spectrum Cook-Book will be published that will include new Cuisine Sections and new recipes for Existing Cuisine Sections.

Sources will always be acknowledged and back-ground tradition encouraged.

There will always be fresh delights and challenges for those who enjoy their food and drink.

CUISINE SECTIONS

1
Afro-Caribbean Cuisine

There is no distinct trend in Caribbean cooking. The few remaining elements of African cooking enabled the Caribbean people to inherit a legacy which affords as unique, exotic and delectable a cuisine as would satisfy the most demanding gourmet. The plantocracy, as old time wealthy planters were called, were by no means tyrants. They were anxious to keep their labour force contented and healthy, and they imported foods from Africa, Spain, and North America. In very early days soon after discovery by Colombus, European settlers brought crops from the 'Old World'. Some inevitably failed. Fruit, however, immediately flourished. Figs, oranges, and lemons came from Spain, bananas and pineapples from the Canaries together with the Canary Islanders to advise as to their cultivation.

Each Caribbean island derives characteristics from its historical past through conquests and colonisation. In some cases, the islands have changed hands between nations not once, but several times. Some have French, Dutch, Spanish, American or British influences, and the national dishes and favourite recipes of the various Caribbean groups are interchanged and enjoyed by all. The people of the islands are quite rightly very proud of their cooking and spend a great deal of time and care in the preparation of their meals.

A unifying element is the West Indian attitude towards seasoning. Nowadays spices are easily found everywhere, but we still don't take them for granted as people do in countries where they grow. Afro-Caribbean cooks treat them with the sophisticated assurance of familiarity. It is, of course, a matter for the individual whether spices are used delicately or a little heavily. It is very much a question of personal taste.

The wealth of delicious fruit and vegetables, mangoes, avocado pears, coconuts, aubergines, sweet potatoes, and breadfruit plus many others, are all put to exciting use in their recipes.

Fish and meat are given a tropical flavour when cooked with curry powder, spices and pepper sauce. The kebab is a popular form of presenting food which simplifies serving meals al fresco, which has obvious attractions in the Caribbean.

Incorporated in the recipe section are dishes which it is hoped will provide the opportunity to experience some of the most exciting and exotic food from this part of the world.

Soups, for instance, include 'Crabs and Greens Soup', (recipe page 15) which has coconut milk among it's ingredients. There is, of course, an abundance of fish around the islands and their availability has produced dishes such as 'Baked Lobster' (recipe page 17). Meat is often combined with fruit, and this creates delicious combinations, as, for instance, 'Baked Paw Paw with Meat Filling' (recipe page 20), or 'Stuffed Duck with Pineapple' (recipe page 22).

It would be misleading to claim that this cuisine is on a par with the great cuisines of Europe and/or that it is as well developed as some of the long established cuisines of the Orient. Today, however, with many islands newly independent, Caribbean cuisine is beginning to flower. It is a cuisine in the making - experimental, exotic and above all, enticing.

Drinks

Traditionally the normal accompaniment to a meal is one of those delicious concoctions which frequently make use of the extensive range of available tropical fruit, e.g. 'Iced Milk and Paw Paw Frappé', and 'Chilled Coconut Milk and Pineapple'. The more potent drinks are predominantly rum based, such as 'Frozen Dacquiri', and 'Rum Coconut Cream'. These and many others are included in the drinks section. It may be that wine is preferred, and this would in no way detract from the pleasure of the meal. Simply remember, 'the right wine is the one you enjoy!'.

SOUPS

CRAB AND GREENS SOUP

*8 oz (200g) Fresh spinach * 1 1/2 oz. (40g) Butter * 2 oz (50g) Finely chopped onion * 1/2 Teaspoon finely chopped garlic * 1 1/4 Pts. (750 ml) Chicken stock * 6 Tablespoons coconut milk (See page 47 for details) * 1 Teaspoon salt * Freshly ground black pepper * 8 oz (200g) Fresh crabmeat*

Serves 6
Wash the spinach under cold running water, discard any coloured leaves bunch leaves together and shred into fine strips. Melt the butter over a moderate heat in a large heavy pan. Add the onions and garlic and cook for 5 minutes, stirring frequently until they are soft and transparent but not brown. Add the greens and turn them about with a spoon for about 5 minutes until they glisten with butter and become somewhat limp. Stir in the stock, coconut milk, salt, and a few grindings of pepper. Bring to the boil over a high heat, reduce the heat to low, and simmer uncovered for about 10 minutes, until the greens are tender. Add the crabmeat and stir for 2 to 3 minutes to heat the crab through. Taste for seasoning and serve up once from a heated tureen.

AVOCADO PEAR SOUP

*1 Tablespoon flour * 1 Tablespoon butter * 1/4 Pt. (1.5 ml) Milk * 1 Pt. (6 ml) White stock * 1/2 Large pear, peeled and pounded * 1 Teaspoon salt * 1/4 Green pepper*

Melt the butter, stir in the flour but avoid browning. Add the milk gradually and cook the mixture until it is a thick white sauce. Stir in the stock. Just before serving, stir in the pounded pear. Warm the soup for a few minutes, but avoid boiling. Season, strain and serve at once.

JELLIED ORANGE CONSOME

*1 1/2 Pints (900ml) Chicken stock * 1/2 oz (13g) Powdered gelatine * 2 Egg whites, beaten * 1 1/4 Pts (750ml) Sprinkled fresh orange juice * Salt * 1 Unpeeled orange, cut crosswise with paper thin slices*

Serves 6

Put stock into a deep bowl, sprinkle the gelatine on top, and let it soften for 5 minutes. Then pour the stock into a large, heavy saucepan and add the beaten egg whites. Bring the stock to the boil over a high heat, stirring constantly with a whisk. When the stock begins to froth and rise, remove the pan from the heat. Let the mixture rest for 5 minutes, then pour it into a large sieve set over a deep bowl and lined with a double thickness of cheesecloth.
Allow the liquid to drain through without disturbing it at any point. Then stir in the strained orange juice, taste the soup and season with salt if desired. Refrigerate the consommé for at least 5 hours, until it is thoroughly chilled and firm enough to hold its shape lightly in a spoon. Serve in chilled soup plates and garnish with orange slices.

RED PEA SOUP

*1 lb (450g) Red Beans (Mexican Chilli beans) * 3 Pints (1800 ml) Water * 1/4 lb (100g) Salt pork, diced * 1 Medium onion, finely chopped * 3 Sprigs parsley * 1/2 Teaspoon dried thyme * Small celery stalk with leaves * 1 Hot red pepper, seeded & chopped * Salt*

Serves 4

Wash the beans thoroughly drain, and put on to cook with 3 pints water, salt pork, onion, parsley, thyme, celery and red pepper. Cover, and simmer until the beans are very tender, about 2 1/2-3 hours. Remove the parsley, and celery. Puree the soup quickly in a blender. The puree should retain some texture. Return soup to the saucepan and season with salt to taste.

FISH

BAKED LOBSTER

*1 3/4 (700g) Lobster, cut into 1 inch chunks * Juice of 2 large limes * 5 oz (125g) Unsalted butter * 2 Medium onions, finely chopped * 2 Cloves garlic, finely chopped * 1 Tablespoon fresh hot red pepper seeded and chopped * 3 oz (75g) Freshly made breadcrumbs * Salt and pepper * 2 Teaspoons Worcestershire sauce * Lime wedges*

Serves 4
Mix the lobster with the lime juice and leave for 15 minutes. Heat all but 1 oz of the butter in a heavy 10 inch frying pan and sauté the onions lightly with the garlic and peppers until the onions are tender but not browned. Add 2 oz (57g) of the breadcrumbs and cook, stirring from time to time until the crumbs are golden. Add the lobster and lime juice season to taste with salt, pepper and Worcestershire sauce and turn into a buttered 1 1/2 Pt. (850ml) soufflé dish. Top with the remaining breadcrumbs and dot with remaining butter. Bake in a preheated 350 degrees F, 150 C, Gas 4 for half an hour or until the top is golden. Serve with lime wedges.

CRAB PILAU

*1 lb (450g) Tinned or frozen crabmeat * 3 Tablespoons lime juice * 2 Tablespoons vegetable oil * 1 oz (25g) Unsalted butter * 2 Medium onions, finely chopped * 1 Clove garlic, chopped * 1 Fresh hot pepper, seeded chopped * 2 Tablespoons curry powder 1 lb (450g) Long grain rice * 1 1/2 Pts. (850 ml) Coconut milk Salt, pepper * 1 Tablespoon chopped chives*

Serves 6
Put the crabmeat into a bowl, add the lime juice and set aside. In a heavy casserole, heat the oil and butter and sauté the onions, garlic and pepper until the onions are tender but not browned. Add the curry powder and cook, stirring for 3 or 4 minutes, being careful not to let the powder burn. Stir in the rice and cook for about a minute longer, just to coat the grains. Add the coconut milk, season to taste with salt and pepper, stir, and cook, covered, over a low heat until the rice is almost done, about a quarter of an hour. Fold in the crab meat and any liquid and the chives. Cover and cook for about 5 minutes longer, or until all the liquid is absorbed and the crab is heated through.

FRIED FROGS' LEGS

*12 Pairs medium sized frogs legs * 1 Medium onion, grated * 1/2 Teaspoon ground cloves * 1 Teaspoon salt * 1/2 Teaspoon white pepper * 1 Tablespoon malt vinegar * 1/3 Pint (285 ml) * Vegetable oil * 4 oz (115g) Flour * Lime wedges*

Serves 6

Mix together the onion, garlic, cloves, salt & pepper and vinegar in a large mixing bowl. Add the frogs' legs and allow to stand for 1 1/2 hours, turning the frogs legs from time to time. Heat the oil in a heavy frying pan. Pat the frogs' legs dry with paper towels and dip in flour. Fry half a dozen or so at a time, for about 5 minutes on each side. Drain on paper towels and serve with lime wedges.

HERRING GUNDY

*2 lb (150 kg) Salt herring * 2 lb (150 kg) Potatoes * 2 Medium onions, finely chopped * 1 Teaspoon finely chopped red peppers * 3 oz (85g) Small pitted green olives, finely chopped * 4 Medium diced cooked beetroot * 4 Medium grated carrots * 4 Hard boiled eggs * 8 Fl ozs Salad oil * 3 Tablespoons malt vinegar * Freshly ground pepper * Parsley sprigs * Lettuce leaves*

Serves 6

Wash the herrings, drain and soak overnight in cold water. Drain, pat dry with paper towels, remove the skin and bones, and put the fish through the coarse blade of a food mill. Cook potatoes until tender in salted water, drain, mash and combine with herring. Add the onions, red pepper, olives, 1/3 of the beetroot, 1/4 of the carrot and one of the eggs finely chopped. Add the oil, vinegar and a generous amount of freshly ground pepper. Mix well. Mound on a serving platter and surround with small heaps of diced beetroot, grated carrot and chopped egg. Garnish with sprigs of parsley and lettuce leaves.

PRAWN AND POTATO CAKES

*2 Medium sized baking potatoes, peeled & quartered * 2 oz (50g) Butter cut into 1/2 inch pieces * 1 oz Butter * 4 oz Freshly grated Munster cheese * 1 Egg yolk * 3 Tablespoons chopped fresh parsley * 1 1/2 Tablespoons salt * 1/4 Teaspoon white * 1 lb Raw prawns in their shells * 4 oz (100g) Finely chopped onions 2 oz (50g) Flour * 1 Egg lightly beaten * 1 oz (25g) Soft fresh white breadcrumbs * Vegetable oil * Seasoning*

Approximately 14
Drop the potatoes into enough lightly salted boiling water to cover them completely, and cook briskly, uncovered until they are tender. Drain into a sieve or coriander, return them to the pan and slide the pan back and forth over a moderate heat until dry. Force the potatoes through a slicer over a deep bowl and mash. Add the butter pieces, the cheese, egg yolk, parsley, salt and pepper and beat vigorously using a large wooden spoon until the mixture is smooth. Cover bowl with foil and set aside. Shell the prawns, and clean, chop coarsely. Melt the remaining ounce of butter over a moderate heat in a heavy medium sized frying pan. When foam begins to subside drop in the onions and cook for about 5 minutes, stirring constantly, until they are soft and transparent. Add the prawns and stir for 2-3 minutes, until they begin to turn pink. Do not overcook. Add the contents of the pan to the potato mixture and stir together. Taste for seasoning. To form each prawn cake, flour your hands lightly, scoop up about 2 1/2 tablespoons of the mixture, and shape it into a cylinder about 2 inches long and 3/4 inch in diameter. Roll the cylinder in flour and gently brush off the excess. Paint the entire surface with beaten egg, then dip it into the breadcrumbs. Place them side by side on greaseproof paper as they are shaped and coated. Refrigerate for at least 30 minutes. Fill a deep frying pan with oil to a depth of 3-4 inches and heat to 375 degrees F. Fry in the oil 4 or 5 at a time turning them over and over with a perforated spoon until golden brown. Transfer to kitchen paper to drain.

MEAT AND POULTRY

BAKED PAW PAW WITH MEAT FILLING

*5-6 lb (2.75 kg) Paw paw, cut lengthways in half and seeded * 2 1/2 Tablespoons vegetable oil * 2 oz (50g) Finely chopped onions * 1/2 Teaspoon finely chopped garlic * 1 lb (450g) Lean minced beef * 4 Medium firm tomatoes, peeled seeded, and finely chopped * 1 Teaspoon finely chopped hot chillis * Teaspoon salt * Freshly ground black pepper * 3 Tablespoons freshly grated parmesan*

Serves 6

Preheat oven to 350 degrees F, 150 degrees C, Gas 4. Heat the oil over a moderate heat in a large heavy frying pan until a light haze forms above. Drop in the oil, onions and garlic, and cook for about 5 minutes stirring frequently, until they are soft & transparent, but not brown. Stir in the bay and cook until all traces of pink disappear, mashing it up with a spoon to break away lumps. Add the tomatoes, chillies, salt, and a few grindings of pepper. Cook briskly, stirring occasionally, until most of the liquid in the pan has evaporated and the mixture is thick enough to hold its shape almost solidly in the spoon. Taste for seasoning. Spoon the meat mixture into the Paw Paw shells, spreading out and smoothing the filling with a fish slice. Place the shells side by side in a shallow roasting tin. Set the tin in the middle of the oven and pour in enough boiling water to come about 1 inch up the sides of the paw paw. Bake for 1 hour then sprinkle each with 2 1/2 teaspoons of the parmesan, and bake for about 30 minutes until the paw paw shows no resistance when pierced with the point of a small knife and the cheese is delicately browned. Transfer to a serving dish and sprinkle with rest of cheese.

CREOLE RABBIT

*2 2lb (2.75g) Rabbits, cut into serving pieces * 4 oz (100g) Salt pork cut into cubes * 1 Onion, finely chopped * 2 Cloves garlic, chopped * 2 Tablespoons brandy * 1/4 Pt. (150 ml) Dry sherry * 1/2 lb (225g) Peeled and chopped tomatoes * 1 Tinned pimento, chopped * 1 Tablespoon of juice from the tin * 1 Green pepper, seeded & chopped * 1 Bay leaf * 1/4 Teaspoon oregano * 1/2 Pt. (300 ml) Chicken or rabbit stock * Salt and pepper to taste*

Serves 6

In a heavy frying pan render the salt pork. Sauté the rabbit pieces in the fat until browned all over. Transfer to a heavy, covered casserole. Fry onion and garlic until browned, and add to the casserole. Pour the brandy into the pan, stir and scrape up all the brown bits. Pour over the casserole contents and ignite. Add all the other ingredients, using enough stock to cover the rabbit pieces. Cover the casserole and cook in a 350 degrees F, Gas 6 oven for about 2 1/2 hours, or until the rabbit is tender.

PORT ROYAL LAMB CUTLETS

*6 Lamb cutlets, trimmed * Salt, freshly ground pepper * 2 oz (50g) Unsalted butter * Bay leaf * 1 Tablespoon vinegar * Juice of 6 oranges * Grated peel of 2 oranges * 1/2 Teaspoon angostura bitters * 1/2 Teaspoon hot pepper sauce * 2 Egg yolks * Chicken stock, if needed*

Serves 6

Rub the cutlets with salt and plenty of pepper. Heat the butter in a heavy covered casserole, add lamb and brown all over. Add the bay leaf, vinegar, orange juice, and grated orange peel, hot pepper sauce, and a little stock if necessary to barely cover the meat. Cover, and cook over a low heat until the meat is tender, about 1 1/2 hours. Remove the cutlets to a serving dish and keep warm. Remove excess fat from the pan liquid and boil to reduce to about 3/4 Pt. (450 ml). Beat the egg yolks lightly and heat in 2 or 3 tablespoons of the hot liquid. Gradually add the egg mixture to the casserole, heating constantly. Do not allow the mixture to boil. When the sauce is thickened, pour over cutlets and serve at once.

DUCK WITH PINEAPPLE

5 1/2 lb (3 1/2 g)
Stuffing: *2 oz (50g) White bread * 1/2 inch cubes* 4 oz (100g)
Unsalted butter * 4 Tablespoons finely chopped blanched almonds
* 2 oz (50g) Seedless raisins * 2 Finely chopped onions
2 Teaspoons finely chopped garlic * Liver of duck * 1/2 lb (400g)
Lean boneless ham, chopped into 1/4 inch dice * 1 Tomato
peeled, seeded and chopped * 2 Tablespoons finely chopped
parsley * 2 oz (50g) Pimento stuffed green olives, chopped
1 Tablespoon capers * Salt and pepper to taste*

Serves 6
To make the stuffing
Heat 2 oz (50g) of the butter in a heavy frying pan and sauté the bread
cubes until crisp and golden brown. Remove with a slotted spoon.
Add the rest of the butter and sauté the almonds for 2 or 3 minutes
until golden, then add onions and garlic and sauté, stirring until the
onions are tender but not brown. Add the duck liver and cook until it is
lightly browned but still pink inside. Remove the liver, chop finely and
reserve. Add the ham and tomatoes to the frying pan and cook until
most of the liquid has evaporated, stirring from time to time. Remove
from the heat, add the liver, parsley, olives, raisins, capers, bread,
cubes, salt and pepper to taste and toss to mix. Stuff the duck with the
mixture. Truss and prick all over with a fork to release the fat. Place
on a rack in a baking pan and roast in an oven preheated to 450
degrees F, Gas 8 for 20 minutes.
At the end of this time remove any fat that has accumulated. Reduce
oven to 250 degrees F - Gas 1/2 and roast for 2 1/2 hours, removing
fat as it accumulates. When the duck is cooked removed it to a
warmed platter and allow it to rest. Meanwhile make the pineapple
garnish. Pat the pineapple pieces dry. Pour off all the fat from the
baking pan, add the butter and sauté the pineapple until lightly brown.
Lift out, and arrange around the duck on the platter. Pour wine,
pineapple juice and stock into the pan, scraping at all the brown bits.
Add the arrowroot and cook, stirring until the sauce is lightly thickened.
Pour over the pineapple or serve separately if preferred.

ROAST PORK CALYPSO

*6 lb (2700g) Loin of pork * 1/2 Teaspoon freshly ground black pepper * 1 Teaspoon salt * 1 Teaspoon ground ginger * 1/2 Teaspoon ground cloves * 2 Cloves crushed garlic * 2 Bay leaves, crumpled * 8 Fl oz Dry Jamaican rum * 1 Pt (600 ml) Chicken stock * 4 oz (150g) Brown sugar * 4 Tablespoons lime juice * 2 Teaspoons arrowroot*

Serves 8
Ask the butcher to saw through the bone (the backbone or spine) of the pork. Cut the fatty side in a diamond pattern. Mix the pepper, salt, ginger, cloves and garlic and rub well into the scored surface. Lay crumpled bay leaves on top. Put roast on a rack in a roasting pan with half the rum and 1/4 pint of the stock. Roast in a preheated 350 degrees F, 160 degrees C, Gas 3, oven allowing 30 minutes to the pound. Half way through the cooking baste with a sauce made by combining the brown sugar, lime juice and remaining rum. Baste 3 or 4 times, add more stock to the pan if needed. When roast is done, remove bay leaves, set meat on a platter and keep warm. Spoon all excess fat, measure liquid, add any remaining basting sauce, and bring the quantity up to 3/4 pint (450 ml) by adding remaining stock. Bring to the boil. Mix the arrowroot with a little water, add to the pan, stirring constantly until the gravy has thickened. Adjust seasoning, pour into a sauceboat and serve with the roast.

TROPICAL CHICKEN

*4 lb (275 kg) Chicken, cut into serving pieces * 3 Tablespoons peanut oil * 1 onion finely chopped * 2 Cloves garlic chopped * 1 lb (450g) Unsweetened pineapple chunks, tinned * 6 oz (200g) Water chestnuts sliced * 1 Red pepper, seeded and chopped * 3 Medium tomatoes, peeled and chopped, or tinned Italian tomatoes drained * Salt and pepper to taste * Chicken stock, if necessary * 1/2 lb (250g) Mange tout * 1 Tablespoon chopped chives*

Serves 6
Heat the oil in a heavy frying pan and sauté the chicken pieces until golden on both sides. Transfer to a heavy covered casserole. In the oil remaining in the frying pan, sauté the onion and garlic until the onion is tender but not browned. Add to the chicken, together with the pineapple and dry juice, the water chestnuts, pepper, tomatoes, salt and pepper, cover and simmer gently until the chicken is tender about 45 minute. Add a little chicken stock if necessary. During the last 10 minutes add the mange tout.

DESSERTS

BAKED BANANAS FLAMBE

*4 Large bananas, peeled and sliced lengthwise * 4 oz Brown sugar
* 3 Tablespoons lime juice * 6 Tablespoons light rum * 1
Teaspoon ground all spice * 2 oz Unsalted butter*

Serves 4
Arrange bananas in a well buttered shallow fireproof serving dish.
Sprinkle with the sugar, lime juice, half of the rum and the all spice.
Dot with butter. Bake in a 400 degrees F, Gas 6 oven for 15 minutes,
basting 2 or 3 times during cooking. At the moment of serving, heat
the other half of the rum, pour over the bananas and set alight.

COCONUT PUDDING

*1 lb (450g) Sugar * 3/8 Pt. (850 ml) Water * 1 lb (450g) Grated
coconut * 4 Egg yolks, lightly beaten * 1 Teaspoon ground
cinnamon * 6 Tablespoons dry sherry*

Serves 6
Cook the sugar and water together to form a syrup at the thread stage.
Add the coconut, then stir in the egg yolks. Add the cinnamon, and
sherry and cook over a low heat stirring constantly with a wooden
spoon, until the mixture is thick. Pour into a flame proof serving dish.
Put under the grill to brown the top. Serve with plain or whipped
cream.

GINGERBREAD

*1/2 lb (225g) Plain flour * 1 Tablespoon baking powder * 1/2
Teaspoon baking soda * 1 Teaspoon allspice, ground * 1/2
Teaspoon salt * 8 oz (200g) Butter, unsalted * 4 oz (100g) Dark
brown sugar * 1/2 Pt. (300 ml) Molasses * 1/2 Pt. (300 ml)
Evaporated milk * 2 Eggs, well beaten * 1 oz (25g) Freshly grated
ginger root * 3 oz (75g) Finely chopped crystalised ginger*

Sift the flour, baking powder, soda, allspice and salt together. Melt the
butter, cool, and mix with the sugar, molasses, milk and eggs. Add to
the flour, blending thoroughly. Fold both the grated and crystallized
ginger into the mixture. Pour into a greased 9" x 5" loaf pan and bake
in a 350 degree F, Gas 4 oven for about 35 minutes, or until a cake
tester comes out clean.

PINEAPPLE MOUSSE

*3/4 Pt. (425 ml) Unsweetened pineapple juice * 1/2 lb (225g) Sugar * 6 Tablespoons cornflower * 6 Egg whites * Pinch salt*

Serves 4
Pour the pineapple juice into a saucepan, and add the sugar. Use a little of the juice to dissolve the cornflower, to the saucepan and cook, stirring constantly with a wooden spoon over a low heat for 5 minutes. Cool. Beat the egg whites with the salt until they stand in peaks. Fold into the mixture, gently, but thoroughly. Turn into a serving dish and refrigerate. Serve with whipped or plain cream.

LIME PIE

*2 Tablespoons cornflower * 3/4 Pt. (425 ml) Water * 1/2 oz (10g) Unsalted butter * 2 Eggs, well beaten * 1/2 Pt. (300 ml) Strained fresh lime juice * 2 Tablespoons finely grated lime rind * 1/2 lb (225g) Sugar * 9 inch Pie dish*

Mix the cornflower to a paste with a little of the water. Add the rest of the water and pour into a saucepan. Cook, stirring with a wooden spoon, over a low heat until thickened. Stir in the butter. Remove from the heat and cool slightly. Stir in the eggs, the lime juice and rind and the sugar. Cook, stirring over very low heat for about 5 minutes, or until the mixture has thickened. Pour into the pie dish and chill. Serve with whipped cream. Can be topped with meringues, if liked.

DRINKS

CHILLED COCONUT MILK AND PINEAPPLE

To make about 1 1/4 pts.

*3/4 Pt. Coconut milk, made from 8 oz coarsely chopped fresh coconut and 3/4 pt hot water. (See recipe page 47) * 14 oz of coarsely chopped fresh pineapple * 6 Teaspoons sugar * Almond essence*

Put the coconut milk, pineapple and sugar into the jar of an electric blender and blend at high speed for about 30 seconds. Until the pineapple is completely pulped and the mixture is reduced to a smooth puree. Pour the entire contents into a fine sieve set over a deep bowl, and lined with a double thickness of cheesecloth. Press down hard on the pineapple with the back of a spoon to extract all its juices, discard pulp. Taste and add more sugar and a drop or two of almond essence if desired. Cover tightly and refrigerate for at least 2 hours, until thoroughly chilled. To serve, pour into tall tumblers with ice cubes.

ICED MILK AND PAW PAW FRAPPE

To make about 1 1/4 Pts.

*1 Medium sized paw paw firm and ripe * 6 Tablespoons milk * 2 1/2 tablespoons strained fresh lime juice * 1/2 Teaspoon finely grated fresh lime grind * 2 oz Sugar * 1/4 Teaspoon vanilla essence * 6 Tablespoons crushed ice * Thin lime slices for garnish*

Peel the paw paw using a small sharp knife. Cut it in half lengthways and scoop out the black seeds, then chop paw paw coarsely. Place the paw paw in the jar of an electric blender and add the milk, lime juice, lime rind, sugar, vanilla essence and crushed ice. Blend at high speed for 20-30 seconds until the paw paw is completely pulped and the mixture is smooth and thick. Pour into tall chilled tumblers and garnish with lime slices. Serve at once.

CREAM PUNCH

6 Medium eggs * 28 oz sweetened condensed milk * Grated peel, lime or lemon * 1 Teaspoon vanilla * Dash angosturas bitters * 1 Pint Trinidad rum

Beat the eggs slightly in a large bowl. Add all the other ingredients, except the rum, and mix well. Add the rum, mixing thoroughly. Serve over crushed ice in punch cups.

MANGOADE

2 Cups chopped ripe mango * 2 oz sugar * 3/4 Pt. Water * 1 Teaspoon grated orange rind * 3/4 Pt. Fresh orange juice * 1/4 Pt. Fresh lime juice

Rub the mango through a sieve. Combine the sugar, water and orange rind in a saucepan and heat, stirring until the sugar has dissolved. Cool and add to the mango puree and fruit juices. Refrigerate, serve in tall glasses over ice cubes.

PEACH DACQUIRI

1 Medium sized peach firm, peel, seed and cut into chunks * 3 Fl oz light rum * 1 Fl oz Cointreau * 2 Fl oz Strained fresh lime juice * 2 Teaspoons castor sugar.

Serve 4
Put the peach, rum, cointreau, lime juice, sugar and ice into the jar of an electric blender and blend at high speed for about 25 seconds, until the peach is completely pureed and the mixture smooth and frothy. Pour into 4 chilled 6 fluid ounce champagne glasses, and serve at once.

RUM FLIP

16 oz Medium dark rum * 4 Eggs, lightly beaten * 3 Teaspoons castor sugar * 4 Dashes angosturas bitters * 3/4 Pint crushed ice * Freshly grated nutmeg

Serve 4
Put the rum, beaten eggs, sugar, angosturas and ice into a mixing glass and place a bar shaker on top of the glass. Hold the glass and shaker firmly together with both hands and shake vigorously. Remove shaker and pour, unstrained into 4 chilled tall half pint glasses. Grate a little nutmeg on top. Serve at once.

2

Greek Cuisine

It is a misconception that Greek cuisine is either of Turkish or Italian origin. It is, in fact, very much an original style and although Greek dishes have Italian or Turkish connotations, the original recipes were Greek.

While Greece was under Turkish rule during four consecutive centuries, Greek cooks were obliged to give Turkish names to their meals. Subsequently such recipes were given new national names, and historians have proved that since the fifth century (during Greece's 'Golden Age'), Greek cooking styles spread throughout the Mediterranean area. Italians, in fact, had been so impressed with the Greek culinary talents that ancient Romans enlisted Greek chefs to prepare their famous banquets. Lucullus, whose name is still used to describe great feasts, owed his reputation to Greek cooking.

The ancient Greeks appreciated fine cooking so much that it was classified as an art and the first cookery book in the world was produced by the Greek Archmtus, whose reputation was so great that he became known as Heriod (head) of the Epicureans, (Epicurean - Epicure today - meaning a person who adores a luxurious and sensitive way of life and has discriminating tastes in food and wine).

Greeks love life, and food and drink and good conversation are very important to them. They often congregate in local tavernas where excellent food and wines are served. These are the places to go to experience really authentic Greek meals. The use of aromatic herbs and fresh vegetables plays a very important role in their cooking, and the correct balance of the ingredients is very important as this will enhance to the full the enjoyment of each delicious recipe. You will find the dishes delightfully different and of quite distinctive flavours.

The countryside of Europe's oldest civilisation blooms with the fragrant lemons so widely used for flavouring. As in ancient times, the landscape is dotted with olive trees, source of the world famous olives and oil that is such an important ingredient of Greek cooking. Olive oil is acknowledged to be the best cooking fat to be found.

Fish in Greece is almost regarded as a divine food. It is prepared in many delicious ways including marinated in wine, herbs or lemon. It is baked under mounds of fresh vegetables or fried and topped with a tasty sauce. It was the Greeks who first discovered that oysters were edible.

It will also be found that vine leaves are used extensively, and the kebab is a popular form of presentation. All kinds of meat are popular with the Greeks, but generally lamb and beef are preferred.

Poultry is another dish that has provided the opportunity for some most exciting recipes, for instance 'Lemon Chicken Oregano' (page 38), 'Pigeons in Wine Sauce' (page 37). Outstanding in the meat dishes are 'Rolled Veal Pot Roast' (page 37) and Beef Stew with Quinces (page 36). These, and many others are included to enable you to enjoy to the full the very real pleasure of authentic Greek cooking.

STARTERS

FISH ROE CAKES

6 oz (175g) Cod's roe * *6 oz (175g) Bread* * *4 Tablespoons flour* * *1/2 Teaspoon baking powder* * *1 Tablespoon chopped parsley* * *1 Tablespoon chopped dill* * *3 Tablespoons chopped onion* * *Olive oil for deep frying*

Serves 6

Scald the roe and remove the membrane. Put in a basin and mash well. Soak the bread in water for a few minutes, squeeze dry and add to the roe. Add the flour, baking powder, parsley, dill and seasoning. Fry the chopped onion in a little oil until it becomes transparent but not coloured, and add to the other ingredients. Mix well with a wooden spoon. Shape into flat cakes, dip in flour and deep fry in smoking olive oil until brown and crisp. Drain on kitchen paper and serve very hot.

LARGE WHITE BEANS IN TOMATO SAUCE

1 lb (500g) Butter beans * *1 Large onion, finely chopped* * *3 Tablespoons olive oil* * *2 Garlic cloves, finely chopped* * *1 Teaspoon oregano* * *2 Bay leaves* * *Salt and pepper* * *Juice 1/2 lemon* * *2 Teaspoons sugar* * *1 Tablespoon dried mint* * *Small bunch of parsley finely chopped*

Serves 6

Soak the beans in water to cover for about 4 hours. (The skins will split but do not worry). Fry the onions in oil until golden. Add the garlic and when it begins to colour add the tomatoes and the drained beans with a little oregano and bay leaves. Barely cover with water and simmer gently until the beans begin to soften, then add salt, pepper, sugar, lemon juice and mint, and cook until they are very tender. This can take less than an hour, or much longer depending on the quality of the beans. Be careful not to overcook or they will fall apart. Add parsley towards the end of cooking. Serve at room temperature. This dish keeps well for several days.

GREEK FRIED MUSSELS

*2 Eggs * Salt and pepper * 4 oz (100g) Flour * 1/4 Pt. (150 mm) beer * Oil for deep frying * 1 lb (450g) Mussels * Lemon slices*

Serves 6

Beat the eggs with the salt and pepper and gradually fold in the sifted flour. Mix well. Stir in the beer and beat well for a few more minutes. Leave the batter to rest for 40 minutes. Get the oil smoking hot in a deep frying pan, dip the mussels in the batter and fry them until golden brown. Drain on kitchen paper and serve very hot. Garnish with lemon slices.

MOCK CHEESE SOUFFLE

*1 Small loaf bread * 4 oz (100g) Butter, softened * 8 oz (220g) Gruyere cheese * 4 Eggs * 1 Pt. (600 ml) Milk * Salt and pepper * 3 Slices ham * 8 oz (220g) Parmesan cheese*

Serves 4

Butter thin slices of bread on both sides. Grease a souffle dish and line with the bread slices. Cover with slices of Gruyere and place the ham on top. Sprinkle thinly with the grated parmesan. Beat the eggs with the milk and seasoning and carefully pour over the dish. Allow to stand for 30 minutes and bake in a moderate oven for about 1 hour, or until the top is firm and golden brown.

SAUSAGES WITH GREEN PEPPERS

*5 Tablespoons olive oil * 4 Large green peppers * 1 lb (450g) Tomatoes * 2 Cloves garlic * Cooked frankfurters * Salt*

Serves 4

Heat the olive oil in a saucepan and fry the de-seeded and finely sliced peppers. Peel and slice the tomatoes and add to the peppers. Simmer covered for 20-30 minutes until a thick pulp. Add the finely chopped garlic, salt and frankfurters cut into small pieces. Cook for a further 10 minutes. Serve very hot.

STUFFED VINE LEAVES WITH EGG AND LEMON SAUCE

*8 oz (250g) Vine leaves * Extra vine or lettuce leaves for lining the pan * 3 Tablespoons olive oil * 1 Pt. (600 ml) Water*
For the Stuffing: *1 1/2 lb (750g) Lean minced lamb *
*Salt and pepper * 1 Large onion, finely chopped * 1 Teaspoon dried thyme * Large bunch of parsley, finely chopped * Bunch of mint, finely chopped*
For the Sauce: *1 Tablespoon cornflour * 3 Eggs * Juice of 1 large lemon * 10 Fl oz (300 ml) Stock * Salt and white pepper*

Serves 8
If you are using fresh vine leaves, remove the stems and plunge the leaves in boiling water for a few seconds. As soon as they change colour and go limp, remove carefully and let them drain. If you are using preserved leaves, pour boiling water over them and soak for an hour, changing the water (use cold water) twice to get rid of the salt. Put all the stuffing ingredients in a bowl and knead well. Line a saucepan with vine or lettuce leaves to prevent the stuffed leaves from sticking. To stuff a leaf, place it vein side up on a plate. Put up to a heaped tablespoon of stuffing in a sausage shape near the stem end. Fold this end over the stuffing, then fold the two sides in and roll the leaf up like a small cigar, tucking in the edges to make a neat package. Squeeze gently and place in the saucepan. Stuff all the leaves the same way and place them tightly together, so that they don't unfold, in circles in the pan starting close to the sides and continuing into the centre. Repeat with further layers until they are all used up. Sprinkle with oil and cover with about 1 pt (600 ml) water. Place a small plate on top to hold the parcels down, cover the pan and simmer over a low heat for about 30 minutes, or until the leaves are done. Test by tasting one. To make the sauce, heat the cornflour with the eggs and lemon juice until the cornflour has dissolved. Heat the stock in a pan adding salt and pepper. Add a few tablespoons to the egg and lemon mixture, then pour this into the pan, stirring vigorously. Continue to stir over a very low heat until the sauce thickens and the taste of uncooked starch has gone. Do not let the sauce boil (a few bubbles do not mean that it is at risk of curdling), and let it thicken to a firm jelly like cream. Serve the Dolmathes hot or cold with the sauce poured over, or serve the sauce separately.

FISH

FISH FILLETS ON SKEWERS

*1 1/2 lb 750g) Thick fish fillets * 16 Prawns or shrimps, cooked and shelled * 1 Small onion, thickly sliced * 2 Small tomatoes, quartered * 1/2 Capsicum, cut into squares * Salt and pepper * Lemon juice * Olive oil * 1/2 Cup dry white wine * Long skewers*

Serves 4
Cut fish into pieces about 1 1/2 inches (40 mm) square. Combine all ingredients in a bowl, cover and allow to stand for several hours in a refrigerator. Thread the fish, prawns and vegetables onto the skewers and grill, brushing occasionally with marinade. Serve immediately on a bed of boiled rice.

FRESH SARDINES BAKED IN VINE LEAVES

*2 lb (1 kg) Fresh sardines * Salt and pepper * Juice 1 lemon * Vine leaves * Olive oil*

Clean the sardines and sprinkle with salt and pepper. Wrap a vine leaf around each fish and arrange on a shallow baking dish. Brush the vine leaves with a little oil and cook in a moderate oven for 20-25 minutes. Remove the leaves and serve immediately. The vine leaves and lemon juice impart a very subtle flavour to the fish, but use fresh vine leaves - not canned.

RAGOUT OF MACKEREL

*2 lb (kg) Fresh mackerel * Salt and pepper * 8 Tablespoons olive oil * Juice 1/2 lemon * 2 Large onions, chopped * 1/4 Pt. (150 ml) Dry white wine * 1 Tablespoon chopped dill * 2 Tablespoons chopped parsley * 4 Tablespoons tomato puree*

Serves 4
Clean wash and cut fish into serving portions. Sprinkle with salt and lemon juice and leave aside. Heat the olive oil and fry the finely chopped onions until golden brown. Add the wine, chopped dill and parsley, tomato puree previously diluted in a little water, and seasoning to taste. Cover the pan with a lid and simmer for 10-15 minutes. Dry the fish and lower into the sauce, which should cover it completely. Cook gently for 15-20 minutes or until the fish is tender and the sauce rich and thick. The dish can be eaten hot or cold.

GRILLED SWORDFISH STEAKS

*2 1/4 lb (1 kg) Swordfish in one piece * 1 Medium onion, grated, and pressed to extract juice * Juice of 1 large lemon * 1 Tablespoon olive oil * 2 Garlic cloves, crushed * 1 Tablespoon coriander seeds, crushed * Pinch of cayenne pepper * Sea salt*
Dressing: *2 Tablespoons olive oil * 2 Tablespoons lemon juice * 2 Tablespoons finely chopped parsley * Pinch of ground cinnamon*

Serves 6
Skin the fish and cut into 6 thick steaks, and put these in a large shallow dish. Mix together the onion and lemon juice, olive oil, garlic, coriander, and cayenne pepper, and pour over the fish. Leave to marinate for about 5 hours. Just before cooking, sprinkle the fish with salt, then grill under a high heat for 4-6 minutes on each side until done right through. Cut the steaks into bite sized pieces, arrange on a large dish, then mix the dressing ingredients and pour over the fish while it is still hot. Serve immediately.

STUFFED PLAICE ATHENIAN

*16 oz Well drained, cooked chopped spinach * 4 oz (120g) Feta cheese crumbled * 6 Teaspoons lemon juice * 1/4 Teaspoon dill * 1/4 Teaspoon pepper * 4 x 4 oz (400g) Plaice fillets * 6 Tablespoons water * 4 Tablespoons dry white wine * 2 Tablespoons chopped parsley * Large pinch paprika*

Serves 4
Preheat the oven to 375 degrees F, 190 degrees C, Gas 5. Mix together the spinach, cheese, 2 teaspoons lemon juice, the dill and pepper. Lay out the fillets and spoon half of the spinach mixture along the centre of each fillet. Roll the fish lengthwise to enclose the filling and place seam side down in an 8 x 8 x 2 inch (20 x 20 x 5 cm) ovenproof dish. Mix together the water, wine, parsley, paprika and remaining lemon juice, pour over the fillets and bake in the preheated oven for 15-20 minutes until the fish flakes when tested with a fork.

MEAT AND POULTRY

BEEF STEW WITH QUINCES

*4 oz (100g) Butter * Chopped onion * 1 1/2 lb (675 g) Chuck steak * 1 1/2 Pt. (300 ml) Hot water * Salt and pepper * 1 1/2 lb (675g) Quinces * 2 Teaspoons sugar*

Serves 6
Melt the butter and fry the onions. Cut the meat into small pieces, add to the pan and brown all over. Pour in the water and add seasoning to taste. Peel the quinces, remove the cores and cut into thick slices. Add these to the meat, sprinkle with sugar and cover the pan with a lid. Cook slowly until the meat and quinces are tender. The quantity of sugar can be varied to taste, but the characteristic of this dish is its sweetness.

ESCALOPES WITH BLACK OLIVES

*1 1/2 lb (675g) Veal escalopes (4-5 fillets) * 2 oz (50g) Butter * 4 Tablespoons olive oil * Seasoned flour * 4 Tablespoons dry white wine * 1 Tablespoon lemon juice * 1 Clove garlic * 1 Sliced lemon * 1 Bay leaf * 2 Cloves * Salt and pepper * Lemon slices * 4 oz (100g) Black olives*

Serves 4
Cut the fillet into portions and pound well to flatten. Heat the butter and oil, dip the meat in the seasoned flour and fry until golden brown, turning once. Add the wine, lemon juice and all the other ingredients except the olives and lemon slices. Cover the pan and cook very gently for 40-45 minutes, or until tender. Add the stoned olives to the pan and cook for a further 2-3 minutes. Place the escalopes on a hot dish and surround with the olives and lemon slices. Strain the liquid into a sauce boat and serve separately.

PORK STEEPED IN WINE AND CORIANDER

*1 1/2 lb (675g) Leg of pork * 1 Tablespoon ground coriander * Dry red wine * Salt and pepper*

Serves 4
Cut the meat into small pieces, put in a basin and sprinkle with salt and pepper and coriander. Mix well and pour in enough wine to cover. Leave for 24 hours. Transfer to an earthenware casserole with a tightly fitting lid and cook in a slow oven for 2 - 2 1/2 hours.

ROLLED VEAL POT ROAST

*1 1/2 lb (675g) Fillet of veal, cut in one piece * Salt and pepper *
2 Tablespoons finely chopped parsley * 2 Cloves garlic * 3 Thin
slices ham * 4 Thin slices cheese * 3 oz (75g) Butter * 4
Tablespoons dry white wine * 2 Teaspoons tomato puree * 1/4 Pt
(150ml) Hot water*

Serves 6
Beat fillet with a wooden mallet or rolling pin until very thin. Sprinkle
with salt, pepper, parsley, and the finely chopped garlic. Arrange the
slices of ham and place the cheese on top. Roll up and tie neatly with
string. Heat the butter in a saucepan and lower in the meat roll.
Brown all over and add the wine and the tomato puree diluted in the
hot water. Adjust the seasoning and cook over a gentle heat until the
meat is tender.

LAMB COOKED IN PAPER

*3 lb (1.5k) Leg of lamb * 1 Clove garlic * 1 Lemon * 1
Teaspoon marjoram * Salt and pepper * 2 oz (50g) Feta cheese
* Butter*

Wipe the meat with a damp cloth, and insert the clove of garlic deeply
into the knuckle end. Rub the meat with lemon juice and the
marjoram, and sprinkle with salt and pepper to taste. Have ready well
buttered greaseproof paper and lay the meat on it. Cut the cheese into
thin slices and put on top of the meat. Wrap greaseproof paper round
it to make a neat parcel and tie with string. Place on a baking tray and
cook in a moderate oven for 2 hours, with cheese side always on top.
Bring to the table in the paper case and serve very hot.

PIGEONS IN WINE SAUCE

*4 Young tender pigeons * Salt and pepper * 4 oz (100g) Butter
* 3 Tablespoons tomato puree * 1/2 Pt. (300 ml) Red wine *
Small piece cinnamon * 1 Teaspoon sugar * 2 Cloves*

Serves 4
Prepare the pigeons and rub well with salt and pepper. Heat the butter
in a skillet and fry the birds until golden. Remove and place on a dish
and split them in two. Dilute the tomato puree in a little hot water and
add to the pan with the wine, salt, pepper, cinnamon and cloves.
Simmer for 2-3 minutes and add the pigeons. Cover the pan and cook
gently until the pigeons are tender and the liquid is reduced to a thick
sauce.

LEMON CHICKEN OREGANO

*4 x 5 oz (600g) Skinned and boned chicken breasts * 3 Teaspoons margarine * 2 Tablespoons lemon juice * 3 Teaspoons olive oil * 2 Garlic cloves * 1 Teaspoon oregano * 1/2 Teaspoon salt * 1/2 Teaspoon pepper*
***TO GARNISH:** 4 Lemon slices * 2 Teaspoons chopped parsley*

Serves 4
Melt the margarine in a small saucepan, add the lemon juice, oil, garlic, oregano, salt and pepper and bring to the boil. Reduce the heat to low and simmer for 1 minute. Transfer to a mixing bowl and allow to cool completely before adding the chicken. Turn the chicken in the marinade, cover, and refrigerate for at least one hour. Transfer the chicken to a shallow baking dish large enough to hold the chicken in a single layer. Brush half the marinade over the chicken and grill for 4 minutes. Turn the chicken over and brush with the remaining marinade, return to the grill for a further 4 minutes or until browned and cooked.

GRECIAN CHICKEN WITH ONIONS

*3-4 lb (1.75k) Chicken, seasoned with flour * 3 Tablespoons olive oil * 40 Shallots or small onions * 2 oz (50g) Butter * 1/4 Pt. (150 ml) Dry red wine * 2 Cloves garlic * 1 Bay leaf * Salt and pepper * Tomato puree*

Serves 6
Wash and dry the chicken. Cut into suitable pieces for serving, dip in seasoned flour and fry in the olive oil until golden. Fry the onions whole in the butter, remove and place in a saucepan. Place the chicken pieces over the onions, pour in the wine and add the garlic, bay leaf, salt and pepper, and tomato puree. Cover well and cook over a very low heat for about 45 minutes.

DESSERTS

DRIED FRUIT FRITTERS

*6 oz (175g) Flour * 2 Teaspoons baking powder * Pinch salt * 2 oz (50g) Sugar * 1 oz (25g) Currants * 1 oz (25g) Sultanas * Lemon essence * 1 Egg * 1/4 Pt. (150 ml) Milk and Water mixed * Oil for frying * Icing sugar * Cinnamon*

Serves 8
Sift the flour, baking powder and salt, and add the sugar and dried fruit. Make a well in the middle and stir in the beaten egg mixed with flavouring to taste, and gradually pour in the milk and water mixture. Beat for a few minutes. Drop spoonfull of the butter in smoking hot oil and fry until golden on both sides. Drain on kitchen paper and sprinkle with sugar and cinnamon.

GREEK HONEY TWISTS

*3 Eggs, beaten * 9 oz (270g) Plain flour * 1/2 Teaspoon baking powder * 1/4 Teaspoon salt * 2 Tablespoons vegetable oil * 2 Tablespoons honey * 2 Tablespoons castor sugar * 1/4 Teaspoon ground cinnamon*

Serves 6
Measure out and reserve 2 tablespoons of the beaten eggs. Sieve the flour, baking powder and salt into a mixing bowl, add the remaining egg, and stir in the oil. Turn out onto a flat surface and knead well until smooth and elastic, 8-10 minutes. Cover the dough and leave to rest for 10-15 minutes. Preheat the oven to 375 degrees F, 190 degrees C, Gas 5. Roll out the dough between two sheets of baking parchment to a thickness of about 1/4 inch (3 mm) to form an 18 x 18 inch (46 x 20 cm) rectangle. Cut into 18 8 x 1 inch (20 x 5 cm) strips. Twist each strip of dough and place on a non-stick baking sheet. Brush each twist with an equal amount of the reserved egg and bake in the preheated oven until golden, 8-10 minutes. Transfer to a wine rack to cool. In a small saucepan, heat the honey, sugar and cinnamon over a medium heat, stirring all the time until the sugar dissolves and the mixture is smooth and syrupy, 3-4 minutes. Transfer the twists to a serving plate and trickle the honey over them. Allowing about 3/4 teaspoon per twist.

GREEK ORANGE COMPOTE

*4 Oranges * 8 oz (225g) Sugar * 1/4 Pt. (150 ml) Water * Strip orange peel * 1 Tablespoon Cointreau*

Serves 4
Peel the oranges and cut into rounds. Remove pith and pips and place them in a glass bowl. Boil the sugar, water and orange peel together until they form a light syrup, add the liquor and pour over the oranges. Add a few tiny slivers of orange zest, and leave the compote until it becomes cold.

GREEK CREAMED RICE

*1 Pt. (600 ml) Milk * Strip lemon peel * 5 Tablespoons rice * 4 oz (100g) Sugar * 2 Egg yolks * 1 Tablespoon milk*

Serves 4
Put the milk and lemon peel in a saucepan and bring slowly to the boil. Sprinkle in the rice, stirring well to prevent it from going lumpy, and when partly cooked, add the sugar. Simmer gently until the rice is tender and the mixture creamy. Remove the pan from the heat. Beat the 2 egg yolks with the 1 tablespoon of milk and stir into the rice. Return to the heat, and just before it reaches boiling point remove again and pour into individual glass dishes. Serve ice cold.

PEARS IN SPICED WINE

*6 Firm pears * 2 Cups dry red wine * 1 Cup sugar * 2 Cinnamon sticks * 3 Cloves * Peel of 1 lemon*

Peel, but do not core the pears, leaving the woody stem on, and set them aside. Heat the wine in a saucepan large enough to hold all the pears. Stir in the sugar, cinnamon, cloves and lemon peel, and simmer uncovered for 3 minutes. Arrange the pears stem up in the pan and baste with the wine sauce. Cook the pears slowly, continuously basting, until they are tender and translucent. Remove them to a glass bowl. Reduce the syrup over a high heat until it thickens and pour it over the pears. Serve chilled.

STUFFED APPLES WITH MERINGUE

*6 oz (175g) Sugar * Little water * 1/2 Lemon * 4 Medium sized apples * 1 Egg yolk * 4 Tablespoons icing sugar * 1 Tablespoon flour * 1/2 Pt. (150 mm) Milk * 1 Egg white*

Serves 4

In a small pan prepare a syrup with the sugar, and a little water and a squeeze of lemon juice. Simmer gently for 10 minutes. Peel the apples, but leave whole. Plunge them in the syrup and see that they are completely covered. Simmer for 5-6 minutes. Drain well, slice off the top and remove the core with a small spoon. Leave aside. Beat the egg yolk with 2 tablespoons of icing sugar, add the grated rind of the lemon and mix in the flour very carefully, so as not to make it lumpy. Warm the milk and gradually add to the egg mixture. Return to the pan and boil up at once. Remove from the heat and cool. Place the apples on a greased tin and fill with the mixture. Whip the egg whites until stiff and fold in the rest of the icing sugar. Put a spoonful on each apple and bake in a moderate oven for 30 minutes.

CHEESES

The Greeks are great cheese lovers, and it is used with carefree abandon. It is a must in Greek cooking. Cheese is a constant ingredient in all kinds of dishes, such as fish, meat, salad and especially appetisers.

FETA
The national cheese of Greece, made from goats' milk. It is excellent on crackers or bread, and is used extensively in cooking. Tangy and slightly salted, it is hard and crumbles easily. It is pure white in colour.

KASSERI
Ewes' milk. Very similar to a young Pamesan. It has a wine taste.

MIZITHRA
Soft and unsalted, made from ewes' milk. It is very similar to cottage cheese.

GREEK GRUYERE
Goats' milk. Delightful nutty flavour.

WINES

Greece is correctly credited with being the birthplace of wine, and Dionysius is the God of Fruitfulness and Wine. It was the Greeks who introduced vines to France in about 600 BC, and taught the people of the Rhone Valley the technique of growing grapes.

SANTA HELENA
White. Dry. Ideal with fish and poultry. Serve chilled. Attractive bouquet.

DOMESTICA
Red or white. Both have refined fragrance and taste. The red is excellent with meat, hare, venison or any robust food.

RODITS
Rose. Bright rosy pink in colour. Serve chilled. Crisp and refreshing.

RETISMA
The typical Greek wine and world famous. Beautiful golden colour. Lovely flavour and fragrance.

MAURO DAPHNE
Red. Served as aperitif wine. Rich and fulsome. Sweet.

CASTEL DANIELIS
Exquisite. Full bodied. Fruity bouquet. Will balance a fine meal.

OUZO
The most famous Greek aperitif, or as an afternoon 'pick me up'. It is distilled from grapes which have first been pressed to produce wine. Various herbs are added, the main one being anise, resulting in a unique taste. Ouzo is a strong drink and though many dilute it with cold water or ice cubes, a true connoisseur will drink it straight. It is always accompanied by appetisers, such as olives, cheese and sausage.

3
Indian Cuisine

Because India is such a vast country its people often pass a lifetime without even tasting the food of other areas, although this no longer applies in large cities and towns which have become increasingly cosmopolitan. There one will find that eating places of different regions have sprung up to cater for the broader spectrum of tastes. On the whole, however, Indians are conservative in their eating habits and hesitant to try different foods.

The regional variations in Indian food are based on a complete fusion of various climates and cultures. Most of the world's religions exist in India. The two principal cultures that have influenced eating and cooking habits are Hindu and Moslem. As each new wave of settlers arrived, they brought some of their own culinary delights, but over the years they have merged with the Indian cuisine and blended the two to perfection. Throughout India, cooking lays great emphasis on herbs - for a description of the most commonly used herbs and spices see page 112.

The Hindus are, by tradition, vegetarian and this has links throughout India, although regional variations have given it diversity. Although many Hindus are no longer vegetarians, their real expertise still lies in cooking vegetarian food. This is reflected in the many variations in the preparation of dals (pulses), vegetables, pickles, and chutneys.

The Muslim tradition of food in India developed after the establishment of the Mogul Empire in the 16th century. Over the following 200 years the tradition of mughali was perfected and is maintained throughout India today. The food is usually cooked in a fair amount of oil (ghee), and is therefore rich. Each region has evolved different methods of cooking.

The Punjabis, for example, have developed Tandoori cookery which is similar to barbecued food, but is cooked in an unglazed clay oven (the Tandoor). In the south steaming is very popular. In the western, central and eastern regions, frying takes precedence over other cookery methods.

The Indian cuisine is based on a combination of flavours and seasonings perhaps more than anywhere else in the world. These encompass hot and sour, hot and nutty, sweet and hot, bitter and salty, etc. It stretches from the freshness and sweetness of highly aromatic curry leaves to the dark pungency of the resin, asafetida, whose earthy aroma tends to startle Westerners just as much as the smell of a strong ripe cheese does Indians.

At most Indian meals vegetables, split peas and rice or bread are served in addition to the meat. There are invariably relishes, yoghurt dishes, pickles and chutneys which round off the full cycle of flavours and textures adding bite, pungency and often vital vitamins and minerals as well.

Curry is, of course, the most famous of Indian dishes. Indian cooks do not use the commercially prepared powder we know, but a combination of herbs and spices, the most usual being cardamom, coriander, turmeric, cumin and ginger. Curry is not necessarily fiery and the 'temperature' can be adjusted from hot to mild. Meat, poultry, and fish are all served in exciting ways with curry such as Special Hussainy curry (page 53), Roast Duck with Spices (page 53), and Curried Pilchards (page 56).

BASIC INGREDIENTS

Besam

Besam is a flour made from roast yellow split peas and can be bought from any shop selling Indian groceries.

Ghee

Use good quality unsalted butter. Heat 2 lbs of butter and melt it in a heavy saucepan over a gentle heat. Heat it to just below boiling point and simmer gently for 30 minutes or so. Most of the moisture will have evaporated by this time and all the sediment will have evaporated by this time and all the sediment will have settled to the bottom. Remove from the heat and carefully strain through a piece of muslin. Ghee can be kept for up to a year in a cool dry place without going rancid. Ghee produces the best results for frying, as the food remains crisp due to the high temperature that can be reached, more so that with any other fat.

Coconut Milk

This is obtained by finely grating the white flesh of the coconut, soaking it in a little tepid water, and then squeezing out the liquid. This liquid is very delicately flavoured and when added to a dish gives a lovely fragrant taste. Cows' milk is no substitute when coconut milk is required.

Garam Masala

*8 oz (225g) Coriander seeds * 2 oz (50g) Cinnamon * 4 oz (100g) Peppercorns * 3 Teaspoon nutmeg powder * 4 oz (100g) Cumin seeds * 2 oz (50g) Cloves * 4 oz (100g) Large cardamoms*

Roast the coriander and cumin seeds separately. Peel the cardamoms. Grind all the spices and store in an airtight container. Use as directed in recipes. Garam Masala can be obtained from shops selling Indian foodstuffs.

Ginger, Garlic or Onion juice

To extract green ginger, garlic or onion juices, pound the required condiment in a mortar after peeling it. Add a dessert spoon of water while pounding. Then put water and condiment in clean muslin and squeeze the juice. Put the squeezed condiment back into the mortar, add 1 teaspoon of water and pound again. Squeeze condiment and water again through muslin into the first amount of juice and the juice ready to be used as desired. If onion is used chop coarsely before pounding.

BREADS

CHAPATIS

*1 lb (450g) Wholemeal flour * Butter*

Mix flour and water to make a fairly stiff dough. Knead very
thoroughly, using a little more water to make a pliable dough. Cover
with a damp cloth and leave for 2 or 3 hours. Knead again. Take
pieces as large as an egg and make into round balls. Flatten the balls
and roll out very thinly into rounds the size of a small plate. Heat
griddle until it is very hot and put a chapati on it for about 1/4 minute,
then turn and cook until brown spots appear. Turn it over and press
gently on the sides with a clean cloth until the chapati puffs up. Take
off the griddle and butter on one side only and serve. To keep soft and
hot, wrap in a clean cloth. All chapatis should be served hot and
preferably as soon as they are cooked.

MILK CHAPATIS

*1 lb (450g) Plain flour * 1 oz (25g) Butter * 3 Tablespoons milk
* Salt*

Mix the flour and salt. Blend in the butter, then knead the whole to a
soft dough with the milk and as much cold water as required. Divide
into 16 parts and roll out each part the size required 1/4 inch (5mm)
thick. Heat griddle white hot, reduce heat and heat gently until nicely
cooked, brown and crisp.

ROGMI ROTI

*1 lb (450g) Wholemeal flour * 3 Tablespoons cream * Salt to
taste * 1/4 Pt. Milk (150 ml) * 2 oz (50g) Ghee*

Sieve flour and add the salt, cream, ghee and milk. Knead the dough
until soft and pliable. Make balls the size of a large egg and roll into
mounds the size of a small plate. Cook on a very hot griddle like
chapatis.

RICE

EXOTIC FRIED RICE

*1 lb (450g) Rice * 4 oz (100g) Ghee or butter * 1 Medium onion
* 2 Teaspoons salt * 1 Small stick cinnamon * 1 Bay leaf * 3
Peppercorns*

Serves 8
Heat the ghee in a large saucepan and add the finely sliced onion. Fry
until golden brown, remove from the pan and keep aside. To the hot
fat add the washed and drained rice and the spices. Keep stirring and
fry for 4-5 minutes until the rice appears glazed. Now add salt and
boiling water. The water should be 1 inch (2.5 cm) above the rice.
Bring to the boil and simmer gently until the water is nearly all
absorbed. Put into a very slow oven for 20-25 minutes until the rice is
cooked. Serve garnished with fried onions.

MASALA KEDGEREE

*8 oz (225g) Rice * 4 oz (100g) Arhat dal * 1/2 Teaspoon turmeric
* 1/4 Teaspoon cinnamon * 2 Teaspoons salt * 2 1/2 oz (65 g)
Ghee * 2 Medium onions * 1/4 Teaspoon ginger * 1/4 Teaspoon
chilli * 1 Clove garlic * 1/2 Teaspoon clove powder*

Serves 4
Wash and dry the rice and dal. Roast them in a moderate oven for
about 10 minutes. Slice the onions finely. Pound the garlic and add to
it the ginger, and chilli. Heat the ghee and fry the onions crisp and
brown. Remove half and reserve. Add to the fat and onions the garlic
mixture, cinnamon and clove. Stir and add the rice and dal and fry for
5 minutes. Add 1 pt (600 ml) hot water, salt, turmeric and simmer
until rice and dal are cooked. Add a little more water if required. Serve
with fried onions sprinkled on top.

PRAWN OR SHRIMP PULAS

*6 oz (175g) Tomatoes * 4 oz (100g) Ghee * 2 Teaspoons garam masala * 1 Teaspoon chilli powder * 1/2 Teaspoon ginger * Salt to taste * 1 lb (450g) Prawns or shrimps * 8 oz (250g) Rice * 2 Green cardamoms * 4 Cloves * 4 Peppercorns * Small stick cinnamon*

Chop the tomatoes. Heat the ghee in a saucepan. Add the tomatoes, garam masala, chilli, ginger and salt, and cook for 5 minutes stirring all the time. Now add prawns and cook over a low heat in a covered pan until the prawns are ready. Boil in a pan 3 pts (1.75 ltrs) water and add washed and drained rice, with the cardamoms, cloves, peppercorns and cinnamon tied in muslin. Boil uncovered until the rice is cooked and drain in a colander. In a fireproof dish put a layer of rice, then a layer of the curry, then a layer of rice. Cover, and put in a slow oven for 10 minutes.

MUTTON BIRYANI

*lb (450g) Mutton * 6 Peppercorns * 4 Green cardamoms * 2 Teaspoons black cumin seed * 6 oz Ghee * 8 oz (225g) Onions, finely sliced * 4 Tablespoons yoghurt * Salt to taste * 2 Teaspoons coriander * 1 Teaspoon chilli powder * 1 lb (450g) Rice * 2 Bay leaves * 2 oz (50g) Blanched almonds*

Serves 8
Cut meat in 1 1/2 inch (4 cm) pieces. Grind the peppercorns, cardamoms, and half the cumin seeds. Heat 3 oz (75g) ghee, fry the onions until a light brown. Take out half the onions and keep aside. Put the meat, yoghurt and salt into the pan with the onions and simmer until the meat is cooked and is a rich brown. Stir occasionally while cooking. Add the ground spices, coriander and chilli and fry over a low heat for a few minutes until well mixed. Take a large pan which can fit into the oven and heat 3 oz (75g) ghee in it. Add the washed and drained rice, and bay leaves and fry for 4 minutes. Add the cumin, onions, and salt, and fry some more. Take out nearly all the rice, leaving a layer at the bottom of the pan. Put a layer of meat onto this, then a layer of rice and so on, ending with a top layer of rice. Decorate with blanched almonds. Add enough water to come 1 inch (2.5 cm) above the level of the rice. Put on the heat and bring to the boil, simmer until the water has evaporated. Put in a slow oven for 20 minutes.

MEAT AND POULTRY

BOMBAY CHICKEN CURRY

*4 lb (1.75 kg) Chicken, jointed * 2 Tablespoons vinegar * 4 oz (100g) Desiccated coconut * 4 Cloves garlic * 1/2 Teaspoon cumin powder * 1/2 Teaspoon turmeric * 1 Teaspoon chilli powder * 1/2 Teaspoon freshly ground pepper * 2 Tablespoons olive oil * 1 Teaspoon ginger * 10 Curry leaves * 2 Teaspoons salt * 3 Teaspoons sugar*

Serves 4
Boil the chicken (in a pressure cooker if possible). Mix or grind together with the vinegar, the coconut, garlic, cumin, turmeric, chilli and pepper. Heat the oil in a saucepan and gently fry all the mixed spices. Add the ginger and 1/2 Pt. (300 ml) stock. Simmer for 15 minutes, then add the salt and sugar and remove from the heat after stirring. Can be eaten hot or cold.

PORK VINDALOO

*2 lb (1 kg) Pork * 3 Large onions * 5 Cloves garlic * 2 Large cardamoms * 8 Cloves * 20 Peppercorns * 3 Tablespoons vinegar * 3 Teaspoons chilli powder * 1 Teaspoon cinnamon powder * 2 Teaspoons cumin powder * 2 Teaspoons turmeric powder * 2 Teaspoons mustard powder * 1 Teaspoon ginger powder * Salt to taste * 4 Tablespoons mustard oil*

Serves 6-8
Grind 2 onions, garlic, cardamom seeds, cloves and peppercorns to a paste with a little vinegar. Mix into this paste all the powdered spices. Add vinegar to keep moist. Wash, dry and cut pork in 1 1/2 inch (4 cm) pieces. Put meat into a bowl and marinate the pieces with a quarter of the paste and salt to taste. Pour all the vinegar over the meat and leave for 5-6 hours. Slice the remaining onion finely. Heat the oil until it smokes, then cool. Put on a medium heat and fry the onions until light brown, add the masala paste and fry until the raw smell disappears. Add the pork mixture and simmer over a low heat until the meat is tender. This is a very hot curry and can be kept for a few days. No water must be used when cooking the vindaloo.

INDIAN CHICKEN AND TOMATOES

*2 1/2 lb (1.25 kg) Chicken * 1 Large onion * 3 Cloves garlic *
1/2 Teaspoon sugar * 1 Tablespoon vinegar * 2 oz (50g) Ghee *
1/2 Teaspoon ginger powder * 1 1/2 (675 g) Tomatoes * 9
Teaspoons garam masala * Salt to taste*

Serves 4
Slice the onion and garlic finely. Dissolve the sugar in the vinegar.
Heat the ghee and fry the onions, garlic and ginger for 5 minutes. Add
the jointed chicken and fry until browned, stirring so that they do not
stick to the pan. Add 3 1/2 pts hot water and simmer until the
chicken is tender and just 1/2 pt (300 ml) of gravy remains. Now add
the halved tomatoes and simmer until half the liquid is dissolved. Add
the garam masala, salt and vinegar. Bring to the boil, cook for 3
minutes more. Serve hot.

MEAT CURRY

*2 lb (kg) Lean meat * 1 lb (450g) onions * 4 Cloves garlic * 1
Teaspoon turmeric * 1 Teaspoon cumin * 2 Teaspoons coriander
* 1 Teaspoon ginger * 2 Teaspoons chilli * 1 Teaspoon paprika
* 2 Teaspoons poppy seeds * 4 oz (100g) Ghee * Salt to taste *
2 Bay leaves * 8 oz (225g) Tomatoes * 1 Teaspoon garam masala*

Serves 6
Wash, dry and cut meat in 1 inch (2.5 cm) cubes. Slice 8 oz (225 g)
onions finely. Grind 8 oz (225 g) onions and garlic to a paste. Add to
the paste 1 dessert spoon of water and mix in the turmeric, cumin,
coriander, ginger, chilli and paprika powders, grind the poppy seeds
and add to the paste. Heat the ghee and fry the sliced onions, golden
brown. Lower heat, add the paste and fry for 3-4 minutes, stirring all
the time. Add the meat and the salt and increase the heat and fry for 5
minutes. Add the bay leaves and tomatoes (quartered). Mix
thoroughly, cover and simmer until the meat is almost tender. Add
garam masala and fry for 2-3 minutes. Cover and simmer until ready.
If the liquid dries up while cooking, add hot water, 2 tablespoons at a
time. Stir often so that the curry does not stick to the pan. Serve with
rice or bread.

ROAST DUCK WITH SPICES

*1 Small duck * 2 Large onions * 2 Green chillies * 4 Thick slices bread * Milk, sufficient to soak bread * 8 oz (225 g) Mashed potatoes * 1/2 Teaspoon ginger * Salt to taste * 1/2 Teaspoon garam masala * 1/2 Teaspoon turmeric * 1 Teaspoon black pepper * 2 oz (50g) Ghee*

Serves 4
Chop the onions, chillies and duck giblets. Remove the crusts from the bread and soak the slices in milk. Mix together the potatoes, bread, ginger and the chopped ingredients. Add salt and garam masala and mix. Stuff the duck with the mixture. Make a paste with the turmeric, pepper, salt and water, and smear on the duck. Preheat a low-moderate oven. Melt the ghee and pour over the duck. Roast it in an uncovered pan, allowing 20-30 minutes per 1 lb (0.5 kg). Baste with its own juices.

SPECIAL HUSSAINY CURRY

*2 lb (1 kg) Lean stewing steak * 1 1/2 inch (4 cm) Piece green ginger * 3 Small onions * 2 oz (50g) Cooking fat * 2 Teaspoons cumin * 2 Teaspoons coriander * 1/2 Teaspoon chilli * 1/2 Teaspoon turmeric * 1 Tablespoon tomato puree * 1/4 Teaspoon salt * 4 Tablespoons yoghurt*

Serves 6
Boil the mutton in one piece until fully cooked. Cut into small squares. Cut the green ginger and onions in rounds. Take a skewer and string onto it one piece of onion, one of mutton and one of green ginger. Repeat until each skewer is filled. Place aside. Now make the gravy of spices. Put the cooking fat into a pan and heat. Mix spices and tomato puree with 1/4 pt (150 ml) water. Put into the pan and fry, stirring all the time, until brown in colour. Season with salt. Add the skewers of meat and the yoghurt.

SPICED CRUMB CHOPS

*8 Lamb chops * 4 Cloves garlic * 1/2 Teaspoon ginger * 1/4 Teaspoon chilli * 1/4 Teaspoon cumin * 1 Teaspoon coriander * 1 1/2 Tablespoons vinegar * 2 Teaspoons salt * 2 Eggs * Breadcrumbs * 2 oz (50 g) Cooking fat*

Serves 8
Place chops between clean tea towels and pound with meat tenderiser. Grind or mince very finely, the garlic. Mix the garlic and spices with the vinegar. Add salt and the chops and leave to soak for 4 hours. Egg and breadcrumb the chops. Fry in the fat until brown then put in a casserole. Cover and place in a preheated hot oven for 10 minutes.

SPICED CHICKEN COOKED IN YOGHURT

*2 1/2 lb (1 1/2 kg) Chicken * 1 Large onion * 3 Cloves garlic * 1 Teaspoon ginger powder * 2 oz (50g) Ghee * 1 Teaspoon salt * 3/4 Pt (450 ml) Yoghurt * 1 Bunch coriander leaves * 1/4 Green pepper * 1/2 Teaspoon turmeric * 1 Teaspoon garam masala * Breadcrumbs * 2oz (50 g) Cooking fat*

Serves 4
Wash and joint the chicken. Slice the onion finely. Grind the garlic to a paste and mix with the ginger powder. Heat the ghee and brown the onion. Add the garlic and ginger paste and salt and cook for 5 minutes. Now add the chicken and brown well. Add 1 1/2 Pts (900 ml) hot water and simmer until the chicken is tender and about 4 tablespoons of gravy remain. Add the yoghurt and the coriander leaves, the sliced green pepper, turmeric and garam masala and stir thoroughly. Bring to the boil and remove at once.

SPICY AND SOUR MEAT

*1 lb (450g) Meat * 3 Cloves garlic * 2 Medium onions * 1/2 Teaspoon garam masala * 1/4 Teaspoon ginger * 1/2 Teaspoon turmeric * 2 Teaspoons cumin * 3 Tablespoons vinegar * 1 oz (25g) Cooking fat*

Serves 4
Cut meat into cubes. Crush garlic cloves and mix with sliced onion and other spices and 2 tablespoons of vinegar. Heat the cooking fat and fry the mixture for 5 minutes, stirring constantly. Put in the meat cubes and fry until brown, stirring constantly to prevent burning. Add the rest of the vinegar to the water and pour into the fried meat and spices. Cover and simmer on a very low heat until the meat is tender. Watch and stir now and again so that the meat does not burn.

FISH

BENGALI FISH CURRY

*1 lb (450g) Fish cutlets * 1 Teaspoon mustard seeds * 1 medium onion * 3 Green chillies * 3 Tablespoons mustard oil or any other cooking oil * Salt to taste * 1/2 Teaspoon turmeric*

Serves 4
Wash and dry the fish. Grind the mustard seeds into a paste. Chop onion and green chillies. Heat the oil and fry the fish. Add onions and chillies and salt. Fry for 3 minutes. Mix the mustard paste and turmeric in 1/2 pt (300 ml) water and add to the fish. Cook until fish is tender.

PRAWN MALLAI CURRY

*1 lb (450g) Prawns * 8 oz (225g) Freshly grated coconut * 2 Onions * 1/2 Teaspoon ginger * 1/2 Teaspoon turmeric * 1/2 Teaspoon garam masala * 2 oz (50g) Ghee * Salt to taste * 1 Teaspoon sugar * 1 Tablespoon treacle*

Serves 4
Steep coconut in 1/2 pt. (300 ml) hot water. Squeeze, strain. Clean the prawns and remove the black thread. Wash and drain them. Slice one onion finely. Grind the other onion to a paste and add it to the ginger, turmeric and garam masala. Heat the fat and fry the prawns. Remove and keep aside. In the same fat fry the sliced onions until golden. Add the onion and spice paste, salt and sugar and fry until the paste is nicely browned. Add the prawns and the coconut milk. Cook until the prawns are tender. Add the treacle and serve.

CURRIED PILCHARDS

*1 lb (450g) Can pilchards * 2 Onions * 1 Clove garlic * 1 Teaspoon coriander * 1/2 Teaspoon cumin * 1/4 Teaspoon ginger * 1 Teaspoon turmeric * 1 Teaspoon chilli * 2 Tomatoes * 2 oz (50g) Ghee * 2 Green chillies * Salt to taste * 1 Teaspoon garam masala*

Serves 4
Slice one onion finely. Grind the other onion and the garlic to a paste. Add all the spice powders except the garam masala to the paste with a little water to keep it moist. Chop the tomatoes. Heat the ghee and fry the onion until brown. Add the paste and fry over a low heat for 5 minutes. Add the tomatoes, cover and cook for another 5 minutes. Add the fish, green chillies and salt. Cover and simmer until the fish is heated right through. Sprinkle with garam masala and serve.

GREEN PEPPERS STUFFED WITH SHRIMPS

*2 Large cartons of potted shrimps * 4 Large green peppers * 5 Cloves of garlic * 1/2 oz (15g) Cooking fat * 1/4 Teaspoon ginger * 1/4 Teaspoon chilli * 1/2 Teaspoon paprika * 1 Teaspoon salt * 1/2 Teaspoon cumin * 1/4 Teaspoon turmeric * 6 Large onions*

Serves 4
Cut the green peppers in half. Take out the seeds and the knob of flesh at the top. Scald in hot water and set aside. Chop the garlic very fine. Heat the cooking fat in a frying pan and fry the garlic, ginger, chilli, paprika, salt, cumin and turmeric for 5 minutes. Then add the shrimps and onions, stirring the mixture now and then so that it does not burn. Turn the flame low and cover the pan. Simmer until shrimps are soft. Stuff into the peppers. Place the peppers carefully in a greased ovenproof dish. Place the dish in a roasting pan containing hot water. Put in preheated oven for half an hour.

INDIAN FISH KEBABS

*2lb (1 kg) Firm fleshed fish * 2 Cloves garlic * 4 oz (100g) Onions
* 1/4 Pt. (150 ml) Yoghurt * Salt to taste * 1/2 Teaspoon ginger
* 1 Teaspoon chilli powder * 2 Teaspoons garam masala *
Melted butter for tasting*

Serves 6
Cut the fish into cubes. Grind the garlic and add it to the bowl of water
in which the fish is to be washed. Wash and drain the fish cubes.
Grind the onions and mix with the yoghurt, salt and spices. Marinate
the fish in it for 2 hours. Thread the fish onto skewers and grill. Brush
with melted butter while grilling.

INDIAN ROASTED SPICED FISH

*2 lb (1 kg) Whole fish * 1/4 Green pepper * Bunch of coriander
leaves * 1 Teaspoon cumin * 1/4 Teaspoon chilli * 1/2
Teaspoon ginger * 1/2 Teaspoon garlic salt * 1 Tablespoon garlic
vinegar * 1 oz (25g) Butter*

Serves 6
Chop the green pepper and coriander leaves. Mix all the ingredients
and salt in the vinegar. Stuff the fish with the mixture but rub some on
the fish as well. Butter the fish and tie with string or wrap in tin foil.
Put in greased baking dish and bake in a moderate oven. If baked
unwrapped, baste with butter and turn when red. When fish is cooked,
pour off the gravy and thicken with a little flour or leave gravy as it is.

VEGETABLES

CAULIFLOWER COOKED IN YOGHURT

*1 Large cauliflower * 3 Onions * 2 Cloves garlic * 1/2 Teaspoon
ginger * 1/2 Pt. (300 ml) Yoghurt * 1 Teaspoon sugar * 1
Teaspoon salt * 1 1/2 oz (40g) Ghee * 1 Teaspoon garam masala*

Serves 4
Divide cauliflower into flowers. Slice 1 1/2 onions finely. Mince the
other 1 1/2 onions, garlic and ginger. Put the yoghurt in a bowl, add
the minced ingredients, sugar, and salt and beat with an egg beater.
Marinate the cauliflower in the yoghurt and leave for 2 hours. Make
sure that the yoghurt completely covers the florets. Heat the ghee and
fry the onions golden, add the cauliflower and all the yoghurt and 1/4
pt (150 ml) hot water. Simmer until cauliflower is tender. Sprinkle
with garam masala.

SPICED AUBERGINES INDIAN STYLE

*1 lb (450g) Large aubergines * 2 Tablespoons desiccated coconut
* 2 Tablespoons hot milk * 1/2 Teaspoon sugar * 4 Tablespoons
vinegar * 2 onions * 4 Cloves garlic * 2 Green chillies * 2 oz
(50g) Cooking fat * 1/2 Teaspoon turmeric * 2 Teaspoons salt *
1/2 Teaspoon ginger * 1/4 Pt. (150 ml) Yoghurt*

Serves 4
Wash and cut aubergines into slices. Mix the sugar and vinegar. Slice
the onions finely. Slice the garlic and chillies. Heat the fat and fry the
aubergine slices until brown. Add all the other ingredients and cook
over a slow heat until aubergines are cooked.

DRY POTATOES IN THEIR JACKETS

*2 lb (1 kg) Very small new potatoes * 3 oz (75 g) Ghee * 1 Large
onion, finely chopped * 1 Teaspoon chilli * Salt to taste * 1
Teaspoon turmeric * 2 Teaspoons garam masala*

Serves 6
Wash potatoes thoroughly. Fry the onion until light brown then add
the potatoes, chilli, turmeric and salt and cook for 5 minutes. Cover
and cook over low heat until nearly done. Add the garam masala and
cook until the potatoes are tender.

PARSNIP BHAJI

*1 lb (450 g) Parsnips * 1 Small onion * 1/2 Green pepper * 2 oz (50 g) Ghee * 1/2 Teaspoon turmeric * 1/2 Teaspoon cumin * powder * 1 Teaspoon chilli powder * Salt to taste*

Serves 4
Peel and dice the parsnips. slice the onion. Shred the green pepper. Heat the ghee and fry the onion golden brown. Add the turmeric, cumin, chilli, and the parsnips. Add 3 tablespoons water and salt to taste and simmer until the parsnips are cooked. Garnish with shredded green pepper.

GREEN BANANA CURRY

*2 lb (1 kg) Bananas * 1 oz (25 g) Tamarind pulp * 1 oz (25 g) Desiccated coconut * 1 Tablespoon hot milk * 2 oz (50 g) Mustard seeds * 1 oz (25 g) Sesame seeds * 1/2 oz (15 g) Cooking fat * 1 Teaspoon turmeric * 1/4 Teaspoon chilli * 1 Teaspoon salt*

Serves 6
Soak the tamarind in 6 tablespoons of water for 10 minutes, squeeze and strain the juice. Soak the coconut in the hot milk. Boil the bananas, peel and mash them. Grind the mustard seeds, the sesame seeds and coconut to a paste. Heat the cooking fat and fry the paste, turmeric and chilli for 2 minutes. Add the tamarind juice and bring to the boil. Add the banana pulp and salt. Simmer for a further 5 minutes.

ACCOMPANIMENTS

BANANA AND COCONUT SALAD

*6 Bananas * 2 Tablespoons desiccated coconut * 2 Tablespoons hot milk*

Serves 4
Peel and slice bananas thinly. Soak coconut in hot milk for 30 minutes. Put slices of bananas in glass dish. Pour the soaked coconut and milk over the slices and serve cold.

POTATO BHURTHA

*4 Medium sized potatoes * 1 Large onion * 2 Green chillies * Lemon juice and salt to taste * 1 Teaspoon mustard oil*

Serves 4
Peel the potatoes and dice. Boil in salted water and mash to a smooth paste. Chop the onion and chillies and mix with the potato. Add salt, oil and lemon juice.

CUCUMBER RAITA

*1 Small cucumber * Salt to taste * 3/4 Pt. (450 ml) Yoghurt * 2 Green chillies * 1/2 Teaspoon chilli powder * 1/2 Teaspoon garam masala*

Serves 4
Peel cucumber and grate. Sprinkle with salt and leave for an hour or so. Beat the yoghurt until smooth and if too thick, add a little milk. Chop the green chillies. Squeeze out the water from the cucumber and add the cucumber to the yoghurt. Add the chopped chillies, and taste. If more salt is required, add that also. Put the mixture in a dish. Sprinkle with chilli powder and garam masala and serve.

TOMATO BHURTHA

*4 Ripe tomatoes * 1 Large onion * 3 Green chillies * Salt and sugar to taste*

Serves 4

Scald the tomatoes in boiling water. Remove skins and mash with a fork, removing the hard parts. Chop the onion and the chillies very fine and mix with the tomatoes. Add sugar and salt to taste.

PUMPKIN AND MUSTARD SALAD

*1 lb (550g) Red pumpkin * 1/2 Green pepper * 1 Teaspoon dry mustard * 1/2 Teaspoon ginger * 3 Teaspoons cumin * 1 Teaspoon salt * 1/2 Pt. (300 ml) Yoghurt*

Serves 4

Peel and slice the pumpkin. Chop green pepper very fine. Boil pumpkin, drain and keep warm. Mix mustard, ginger, cumin, salt and green pepper in the yoghurt. Add the pumpkin. Mix well and serve.

CURRIED COTTAGE CHEESE SALAD

*8 oz (225 g) onions * 1 Teaspoon salt * 2 Tablespoons desiccated coconut * 4 Tablespoons hot milk * 1/2 Green pepper * Sprigs of green coriander leaves * 1 lb (450 g) Cottage cheese * Juice of 2 lemons * 1/4 Teaspoon freshly ground pepper*

Serves 4

Peel and slice onions thinly crosswise. Sprinkle with 1/2 teaspoon of salt and rub in with hands. Let stand for 30 minutes, then pour cold water over and drain well. Soak the coconut in hot milk, and let stand for 30 minutes. Chop the green pepper and coriander leaves coarsely. Mix everything together and stir well. Set aside for 30 minutes. Serve cold.

CHUTNEY AND PICKLES

APPLE CHUTNEY

*1/4 Teaspoon ginger powder * 8 oz (225 g) Onions * 2 Cloves garlic * 2 lb (1 kg) Cooking apples * 8 oz (225 g) Brown sugar * 1 Pt. (600 ml) Malt vinegar * 4 oz (100g) Sultanas * 1/2 oz (15g) Mustard seed * 1/4 oz (7 g) Salt * 1 Teaspoon chilli powder*

Mix the ginger with the garlic and onions and grind. Peel and chop the apples. Cook the apples and sugar in the vinegar until the apples are soft. Add all the other ingredients and after bringing to the boil, simmer for 15 minutes or until the mixture is thick and pulpy. Cool and bottle.

MINT CHUTNEY

*12 Sprigs of mint * 1 Onion * 1/2 Green pepper * 2 Tablespoons desiccated coconut * 2 Tablespoons hot milk * 10 Tablespoons yoghurt * 1/2 Teaspoon salt*

Wash the mint. Peel the onion and halve. Wash the green pepper and dry. Chop all three very fine. Soak the coconut in the hot milk for 30 minutes. Beat yoghurt until thin. Add salt. Mix all the ingredients well together. Serve cold.

FRESH RED CHUTNEY

*3 Dates * 1/2 Small onion * 3 Cloves garlic * 1/4 Teaspoon chilli * 1/2 Teaspoon paprika * 1/4 Teaspoon cumin * 1 Teaspoon salt * Teaspoons malt vinegar*

Stone the dates, peel and chop the onion, peel the cloves of garlic. Mix finely all the ingredients except the salt and vinegar, which should be mixed in well after mincing. Serve.

SULTANA CHUTNEY

*1 1/2 lb (675 g) Sultanas * 2 oz (50g) Fresh ginger * 2 oz (50 g) Garlic cloves * 1 oz (25 g) Almonds * 3/4 Pt (450 ml) Malt vinegar * 12 oz (350 g) Moist brown sugar * 2 oz (50 g) Salt * 1/4 oz (7 g) Red chillies*

Wash the sultanas, peel the ginger and cut in thin slices. Peel the garlic cloves and slice in thin slices. Blanch the almonds and remove skin. Soak the sultanas in the vinegar for 24 hours. Then mix all the ingredients in a saucepan, and bring to the boil. Simmer uncovered until vinegar is consistency of syrup. Remove from heat and let it get quite cold. Bottle and cork. This chutney can be eaten next day.

PLUM CHUTNEY

*2 lb (1 kg) Plums * 4 oz (100 g) Green ginger * 2 oz (50 g) Garlic * 2 oz (50 g) Onion seed * 1 oz (25 g) Mustard seed * 1 Pt (600 ml) Malt vinegar * 1 oz (25 g) Chilli powder * 2 lb (1 kg) Sugar * 2 oz (50 g) Salt*

Grind the ginger, garlic, onion seed and mustard seed to a paste in a little vinegar. Stone the plums. Cook the plums and all the other ingredients in the vinegar until thick and pulpy. Cool and bottle.

HOT PEACH PICKLE

*2 lb (1 kg) Nearly ripe peaches * 1 lb (450 g) Brown sugar * 1 Pt (600 ml) Vinegar * 8 oz (225 g) Seedless sultanas * 1 oz (25 g) Chilli * 1 Teaspoon ginger*

Blanch the peaches in very hot water and remove the skins. Split them open with a silver knife and extract the stones. Boil the sugar in half the vinegar. While the vinegar is boiling hot, drop in the peach halves. Simmer until they are quite soft, then add the sultanas, chilli and ginger and the remaining vinegar. Reduce the liquid to desired thickness. Remove from heat, stir well. Let it become quite cold. Bottle and cork. Leave for 2 weeks.

MINCED LEMON PICKLE

*2 lb (1 kg) Lemons * 2 oz (50g) Salt * 1 oz (25 g) Garlic cloves * 1 lb (450 g) Seeded raisins * 1 Teaspoon chilli powder * 2 Teaspoons ginger * 1 1/2 Pts (900 ml) Vinegar * 1 1/2 lb (700g) Moist brown sugar*

Cut the lemon in four, remove the pips and soak with salt in a bowl for 4 days, stirring often. Peel the garlic cloves, soak the raisins, chilli, garlic cloves and ginger for 24 hours in a little vinegar. mince lemons and raisin mixture together. Add the sugar to the rest of the vinegar and mix well. Mix altogether, put in a saucepan, bring to the boil and then simmer until the liquid is reduced and thickened. Let it get quite cold, then bottle. Can be used after 4 days.

DESSERTS

SAFFRON SWEET RICE

*1 oz (25g) Almonds * 1 oz (25g) Raisins * 1/2 Teaspoon saffron strands * 2 Tablespoons hot milk * 1 1/2 oz (40 g) Vegetable cooking fat * 8 oz (225 g) Parboiled rice * 1/4 Teaspoon salt * 3 Cardamoms * 1 inch (2.5 cm) Stick cinnamon * 8 Tablespoons cold milk * 4 Tablespoons sugar * 2 Tablespoons thick cream * 1 oz (25 g) Shelled walnuts*

Serves 4
Blanch, slice and toast the almonds. Clean and fry the raisins. Toast the saffron strands, crumble them and soak in the hot milk. Heat the fat, add the rice, salt and spices and fry for 3 minutes. Add the cold milk and sugar and cook covered until the rice is fully cooked. Now add the cream and sprinkle with the saffron milk. Cover and cook for a minute. Remove to a hot serving dish, sprinkle with almond slices, walnuts and raisins, and serve.

KHEER KAMALA

*2-3 Pts (1.75 ltr) Rich Jersey or unpasteurised milk * Sugar to taste * Rose water * 1 medium can orange segments*

Serves 6
Bring the milk to the boil and simmer on a low heat until the milk becomes very thick. Add the sugar and stir until it dissolves. Remove from the heat, cool and turn into serving dish. Add rosewater to flavour. Drain fruit and add to kheer. Serve chilled.

SWEET POTATO PUDDING

*8 oz (225g) Sweet Potato * 2 Pts (1.15 ltrs) Rich Jersey or unpasteurised milk * 3 Cardamoms * 12 oz (350 g) Sugar * 2 oz (50g) Dals*

Serves 4
Boil the sweet potatoes. Peel and mash them when cool. Bring the milk to the boil and simmer gently until it has thickened slightly. Add the potatoes and simmer until well mixed. Peel the cardamoms and grind the seeds to a powder. Add the sugar, chopped dates and cardamom powder to the milk and cool until thick. Remove from heat and serve hot or cold.

PARSEE BREAD PUDDING

*1 oz (25 g) Almonds * 1 Pt (600 ml) Milk * 3 Tablespoons cream
* 4 Heaped teaspoons sugar * 2 1/2 Teaspoons fresh breadcrumbs
* 1 Egg*

Serves 4

Blanch and slice the almonds into thin slivers. Put the milk, cream
sugar and breadcrumbs into a pan and cook over a slow heat until the
mixture has a consistency of porridge. Stir with a wooden spoon while
cooking. Beat the egg yolk and white separately, and add to the
mixture. Grease an ovenproof dish and put in the pudding mixture.
Sprinkle the top with almonds. Bake the pudding in a preheated
moderate oven for 40 minutes. Watch carefully, as the pudding may
cook quicker and become burnt. If liked, a layer of marmalade may be
spread at the bottom of the dish and a dusting of nutmeg on top of the
almonds.

4

Italian Cuisine

Italian cuisine is one of the oldest in the world. It is derived from Greek gourmet traditions, which in turn originated from oriental cuisine.

Throughout the centuries these culinary skills became firmly established in Italy and gradually attained perfection in the country that adopted them. Italian food is extremely varied and does not begin and end with pasta. Italians have been wonderful cooks for centuries and it was an Italian woman who first won the coveted Cordon Bleu.

Catering in Italy is a family art practiced for, and by the family. The finest accomplishments are not reserved for special occasions or for impressing guests, but are prepared daily for the pleasure of the family.

Once considered the 'poor man's' food, Italian cuisine has been rediscovered and is now appreciated for its simplicity and wholesome qualities. The great strength of Italian cooking is that it makes the most of pure basic ingredients and is relatively straight forward to prepare. At the same time an amazing variety of tastes can be attained by blending and contrasting the flavours of superb raw materials by the addition of herbs and spices and by cooking certain dishes in wine.

The expertise and talents of Italian chefs had a great influence on French cooking, and it was Catherine de Medicis who took Italian pastry cooks and ice cream makers to France. These craftsmen imparted their secrets to their French counterparts.

The range of Italian cuisine is limitless. Apart from pasta dishes for which they are renowned, there are superb chacuterie such as mortadella, salamis, the famous parma ham, zampone, (stuffed pigs trotters), and many others. Great imagination and flair is apparent in meat, fish, poultry and game dishes; choose any Italian dish and it is a replica of one that was enjoyed by gourmands of ancient Rome.

Finally, when dining out in Italy the best cooking is to be found, not in the glittering establishments well known to every tourist, but in the small family run trattorie.

Pasta

This is invariably the first dish that comes to mind when thinking of Italian food and perhaps therefore a brief description would be appropriate.

There is no food that is as simple as pasta. It consists of flour and water or flour and eggs, and can be served in a thousand and one ways. It is a dried wheaten flour preparation usually made from durum wheat; it is mixed with water or eggs into a stiff paste, and then forced through specially designed perforated cylinders from which it emerges in a variety of shapes.

The nutritional value of pasta products is the same as that of the cereals from which it is made. It contains glucides or carbohydrates, mineral salts, a small amount of protein, fats and vitamins (mainly vitamin B1).

Pasta is essentially an energy food providing the body with 350 calories per 100g. It is therefore an excellent staple food.

Pasta is easy to cook but can be spoilt by carelessness. You should never leave the kitchen while pasta is in the pot as precise timing is essential. As already mentioned, there are numerous pasta shapes, and the range of sauces to accompany them is virtually limitless. The sauces themselves provide the adventurous cook with the opportunity to experiment, as it is not necessary to follow recipes slavishly. The various recipes have been selected as an introduction to some of the most popular and best loved pasta dishes, and include, spaghetti, macaroni, tagliatelle, lasagne. All of these will provide great pleasure in preparation and enjoyment in eating; pasta and sauce recipes are on page 73.

Soups

On occasions a pasta course in Italy will be substituted by a soup. Since Italians are great pasta lovers, it is very frequently included in a soup recipe, 'Pasta in Brodo' ('Pasta in Soup'). Minestrone, which is a mixture of fresh vegetables, must be the most famous of Italian soups, but there are very many other superb soups worthy of universal attention (recipes, page 77). In addition to minestrone you will find 'Pasta in Brodo' and a selection of hearty vegetable and meat soups all of which make exciting and tasty eating.

Fish

Italy is a country with a very long coastline so that fish as one would expect features prominently in Italian cooking. Again, with typical inventiveness, Italian fish dishes are among the most highly respected in the world, as they are given quite unique flavours with the clever use of herbs and spices. A selection of recipes has been made which it is felt will enable you to savour some of the finest Italian fish dishes. Included amongst them are, for instance, 'Scampi from Lombardy', 'Tuna from Ligunia', and 'Red Mullett from Trieste'.

Meat

Veal is without doubt the favourite meat of Italy, and it is a rare event indeed to find an Italian menu that does not include at least one veal dish. It is prepared in many appetising ways, and the recipes on page 82 will, it is hoped, give you some unusual but traditional recipes to try. Beef, lamb and pork have increased considerably in popularity over the past few years, and there is a great love of beefsteak. The Italian method of preparing these meat dishes is quite unusual and extremely delicious. None of the recipes (page 83) are difficult to prepare and the results are extremely rewarding.

Desserts

Desserts play a smaller part in Italian cooking than in most other mid-European countries, but they give the cook satisfaction in their love of colour and shape as well as taste. Traditionally most Italian meals finish with fruit or cheese, but when a dessert is served it is frequently a 'torta' (tart) or 'pasticceria' (cake). These are elaborate and mouthwatering concoctions and are frequently flavoured with subtle liquors. These delicacies must be eaten and enjoyed with a complete disregard for the waist line. The recipes on page 87 are predominantly for cakes, but also include such traditional delights such as zabaglione (a type of egg punch), peach fritters and pineapple toast.

Cheese

Next to France, Italy has a greater variety of cheese than any other country. Italian cheeses are among the most famous in the world, including gorgonzola and parmesan, the latter being internationally accepted as the premier cheese for grating and use in cooking.

BEL PAESE

Bel Paese means 'beautiful country' and is one of the best known and most popular of soft cheeses. It is sweet, and mild.

FONDINA

This is one of the most esteemed of the mildest Italian cheeses. It is made with whole milk, semi soft to hard, is yellow in colour and has a delicate nutty flavour and a pleasing aroma.

GORGONZOLA

This is a semi hard blue veined cheese. It is made in round shapes and its excellence depends on the manner of its curing. There is also a variety of white Gorgonzola which is practically unknown outside of Italy, which possesses a slightly bitter flavour and is greatly appreciated by Italian cheese connoisseurs.

MOZZARELLA

Originally made from buffaloes' milk, but cows' milk is now used. As well as being eaten raw it is also the basis for certain pizzas.

PARMESAN

This is a semi-fat cheese with a very slow rate of maturing. Its principal use is in grated form either added to dishes already cooked or to dishes in the process of cooking. It is also used extensively in gratin dishes which require cheese.

RICOTTA ROMANA

A rich creamy and fragrant cheese. It is sometimes taken with sugar, and is for stuffing cannellons and certain types of ravioli.

ROMANO

Sometimes called incontestrato, this is one of the most popular hard cheeses and is made from cows' and goats' milk with a piquant taste. It is suitable for grating.

Wines

The enjoyment of wine is an extremely personal experience, meaning a different thing to each individual. Wine, being a natural and healthy drink, has so great an acceptance in Italy that water is seldom served. An Italian meal without wine is virtually unthinkable. Wine has become so important because of its delicious taste and the unique talent it possesses for enhancing the flavour of food.

Italy is the most prolific wine producing country in the world, and if you are visiting, do take the opportunity of tasting various local wines. You will be surprised at the range of pleasures to be enjoyed.

Obviously a selection of wines is influenced by individual preferences, but it is felt that those listed reflect the best known and most highly regarded Italian wines.

ORVIETO
Very clear, pale golden cast. Dry or semi sweet.

LAMBRUSCO
Red. Normally effervescent. Refreshing. Should be drunk young.

FRASCATI
Dry white. Full bodied and fragrant. Clear golden in colour.

BAROLO
Red. Lovely colour. Strong flavour of violets. Pour with care, can throw a sediment.

CHIANTI CLASSISCO
Light ruby red colour. Fresh fruity. Dry and full of flavour.

BARBARESCO
Red. One of the great wines of Italy. Rich and fragrant.

BARBERA
A ruby coloured wine. Full bodied flavour. Very pleasant bouquet.

VALPOLICELLA
Has an ideal combination of taste, aroma and bouquet.

SOAVE
Straw coloured. Dry and well balanced. Full bodied. Best when very young.

ASTI SPUMANTE
Sparkling white wine. Delicious after dinner. Quite sweet. Pleasing fruity taste of muscat grapes.

PASTA AND EGG DISHES

LASAGNE AL FORNO

*1 lb (450g) Lasagne * 2 Tablespoons olive oil * 1 lb (450g)
minced beef * 1 medium size onion chopped finely * 1 crushed
clove of garlic * 1 Pt. (600ml) water * Salt and pepper * 1
Tablespoon tomato paste * 1 lb (450g) green lasagne or noodles *
12 oz - 1 lb (350-450g) mozzarella or Bel Paese cheese * 3
tablespoons parmesan*

Serves 6
Heat oil in a heavy frying pan add the onion and garlic, and when
slightly browned, add and brown the minced meat. Blend the tomato
paste with a little water and pour slowly over the meat. Cover and
allow to simmer gently for one and a half hours. Cook lasagne in
rapidly boiling water, 5-7 minutes. Grease an oven glass or
earthenware casserole, and in it lay a layer of the cooked lasagne, or
layer of meat sauce and a layer of mozzarella or Bel Paese.
Continue filling the dish in layers until all the ingredients are used up,
finishing with the balance of the sauce poured over the finished dish,
which should be topped with grated parmesan. Bake for 20 minutes in
medium oven.

FLAMING PASTA IN TOMATO SAUCE

*12 oz (340g) Gnocchi * Tomato sauce (recipe page 93) * 3
Tablespoons double cream * 6 Tablespoons vodka * 1 oz (25g)
Butter*

Serves 4
Cook the pasta in plenty of boiling salted water. Meanwhile, heat the
tomato sauce and when it begins to bubble mix in the cream and 1
tablespoon of the vodka. Cook for 2 minutes, stirring very frequently.
Check the seasoning. Drain the pasta, then immediately return it to
the pan in which it was cooked. Toss it with the butter. Then very
thoroughly mix in the tomato and cream sauce. Transfer the pasta to a
heated serving dish. Heat the remaining vodka in a soup ladle until it is
nearly boiling. Bring the dish quickly to the table. Pour the vodka over
the pasta and set fire to it. Toss quickly and serve.

ITALIAN HERB PANCAKES

Crepes: 3 Level teaspoons flour * 1/4 level teaspoon salt * 1
Egg * 7 Fluid oz milk * 1 Tablespoon melted butter * 6 Level
tablespoons finely chopped fresh basil * Butter or oil, for cooking
Filling: 1 Bunch watercress * 1 Head lettuce * 2 Level
tablespoons chopped tarragon * 2 level tablespoons chopped
chives * Butter * Salt and ground black pepper * 1/2 lb (225g)
Ricotta or cottage cheese * 3 Eggs, lightly beaten * 1-2 oz
(25-50g) freshly grated Parmesan * 6 Tablespoons double cream *
Freshly grated nutmeg * 1/2 Pint well flavoured tomato sauce (see
page 93)

Serves 4-6

To make the crepes, sift flour into a mixing bowl. Break egg and add
to dry ingredients. Mix in milk and melted butter, or oil gradually to
avoid lumps. Strain through a fine sieve, add finely chopped basil and
leave to stand at least 2 hours before cooking the crepes. Butter
should be as thin as single cream. Add a little water if too thick.
For each crepe spoon about 2 tablespoons of batter into heated pan,
swirling pan to allow batter to cover entire surface thinly. Brush a
piece of butter on, or around edge of hot pan with the point of a knife
and cook over a medium heat until just golden, but not brown (about 1
minute each side). Repeat until all crepes are cooked stacking them on
a plate as they are ready. The mixture makes 8-12 crepes.

To make filling:

Wash watercress and lettuce. Drain, remove stalks and yellowed leaves
from watercress. Remove outer leaves from lettuce. Chop coarsely.
Combine chopped watercress and lettuce with chopped fresh herbs and
sauce in 2 level tablespoons of butter. Flavour with salt and ground
black pepper to taste. Press dry and then add ricotta or cottage
cheese, together with beaten eggs, freshly grazed parmesan cheese,
cream and nutmeg to taste.

Spread each crepe generously with filling. Roll them and put in a well
buttered rectangular baking dish. Chill until 1 hour before cooking.
When ready to serve, brush each crepe with melted butter. Sprinkle
with freshly grated parmesan, and bake for 20 minutes in a moderate
oven (350 degrees F/180 degrees C/ gas mark 4), serve with a well
flavoured tomato sauce.

ITALIAN SCRAMBLED EGG WITH CHEESE

*6 Eggs * 1 1/2 - 2oz(40-50g) grated parmesan * 2oz (50g) butter
* A little cream*

Serves 4
Beat the eggs lightly, adding a tablespoon of cream. Meanwhile warm
the butter in a small stewpan, pour in the egg mixture, and cook over
moderate heat, stirring continually, until the eggs are scrambled. At the
last moment slip in the grated cheese and serve immediately on
buttered toast.

MACARONI WITH CURRIED CHICKEN

*11 oz (300g) macaroni * 2 oz (50g) butter * 2-3 tablespoons curry
powder * 4 fl oz (110 ml) dry white wine * 2 tablespoons milk *
2 cloves garlic, peeled & crushed * 1 Bay leaf * 1 Tablespoon
sunflower oil * Salt * 1 Tablespoon brandy * 4 Fl oz (110 ml)
double cream * 1 1/2 oz (40g) flaked almonds * 8 oz (225g)
cooked chicken white meat only, boned, and skinned and cut into
strips*

Serves 4
Combine the butter, curry powder to taste, wine, milk, garlic, bay leaf,
oil and salt to taste in a heavy saucepan. Cook over a low heat for 15
minutes, stirring occasionally. Add the brandy, cream, flaked almonds
and all but a few strips of chicken to the pan. Bring to the boil, then
reduce the heat and simmer for 3 minutes, stirring constantly. Remove
and discard the garlic and bay leaf. Check the seasoning, cover and
keep warm.
Meanwhile cook the pasta in plenty of boiling salted water. Drain, then
immediately turn the pasta into a heated serving dish. Spoon over the
sauce, toss well and arrange the remaining strips of chicken on top.
Serve immediately.

SPAGHETTI WITH FRESH FENNEL SAUCE

*1 lb (450g) spaghetti * 4 tablespoons olive oil * 1/2 pint (300 ml) cold water * 6 oz (175g) dried breadcrumbs * 1 tablespoon pine nuts or blanched almonds * 1 lb (450g) dried fennel * 1 large or 2 small onions * 1 lb (450g) fresh sardines * pilchards, or sprats * 1 tablespoon sultanas or Seedless raisins * Salt and pepper*

Serves 4-5
Clean and bone fish. Clean fennel and cook for 15 minutes in 2 pints (1-1.5 ltr) boiling water. Drain, and chop small. Heat olive oil in a stewpan and cook in it the chopped onion until it is golden brown, add fish, cook gently for 10 minutes, stirring frequently. Add fennel, sultanas and nuts, cold water and seasoning, and allow to simmer gently for 10 minutes.
Place breadcrumbs on a fireproof plate below a hot grill for a few seconds to brown. Meanwhile cook the spaghetti (see how to cook pasta page 68). When cooked and drained, place in deep warmed dish, pour over half the fish and fennel sauce and half the breadcrumbs and mix well. Then pile on balance of fennel mixture and top with the remainder of breadcrumbs and serve very hot.

TAGLIATELLE WITH ANCHOVY AND TUNA FISH

*12 oz (350g) cooked tagliatelle * 6 oz (175g) can tunny fish * 3 or 4 anchovies * 1/2 pt. (300 ml) good stock * Salt and pepper * 2 tablespoons olive oil * 1 clove garlic * 1 tablespoon freshly chopped parsley*

Serves 4
Heat oil in a heavy pan, add garlic and cook for 2 or 3 minutes, add tunny and anchovies broken into small pieces or pounded, add parsley stock slowly and bring to boiling point. Pour over cooked tagliatelle and mix well.

SOUPS

ITALIAN HARICOT BEAN SOUP

*8 oz (225g) Haricot beans cooked in water overnight * 1 Clove of garlic, crushed * 3 Pts. (1.75 litres) Water * 1 Tablespoon olive oil * Salt and pepper to taste * 4 heaped tablespoons parsley*

Serves 4
Cover the beans with water, bring to the boil and cook slowly for at least 3 hours. Towards the end of the cooking time, heat the olive oil and add to it the crushed garlic and parsley and cook together for 5 minutes. Pass beans and water in which they have cooked through a sieve or food mill, return to the saucepan, and stir in the garlic mixture. Serve hot with snippets of toast and sprinkle with parmesan cheese.

ITALIAN BROWN LENTIL SOUP

*8 oz (225g) Brown lentils * 1 Onion finely chopped * 1 Clove garlic, crushed * 1 Heaped tablespoon finely chopped parsley * 4 Tablespoons olive oil * 1 Medium sized can tomatoes * Salt and pepper to taste*

Serves 4
The lentils for this soup are the khaki coloured whole lentils not the orange coloured dried lentils. Cook lentils in 4 pts. (2.25 Ltr) boiling, slightly salted water for 1 hour, strain but don't throw away the liquid - and set on one side. Replace liquid in saucepan, bring to the boil and add parsley, onion and garlic, and when boiling furiously add the oil and allow to boil fairly, briskly for a further 10 minutes. Add strained tomatoes, replace lentils and boil gently for 20 minutes more.

MINESTRONE

1 lb(450g) Salt pork, cut small * 4 Pts. (2.25 litres) water or beef stock * 2 Tablespoons finely chopped parsley * 1 Clove crushed garlic * 1/2 oz (15g) Butter * 1 Small cabbage * 2 Carrots, diced * 8 oz (225g) Haricot beans soaked overnight * 4 oz (100g) shelled peas * Few french beans * 4 Tablespoons rice * Grated parmesan * Salt & pepper

Place cut up pork in water or stock and bring to the boil before adding parsley, garlic, chopped vegetables, peas and beans. Allow to boil gently for two and a half hours, then add rice and cook for a further quarter of an hour. Season to taste. Serve with a layer of grated parmesan cheese sprinkled over soup in the tureen.

PASTA AND CHICK PEA SOUP

3 Tablespoons olive oil * 6 oz (180g) onion, chopped * 3 Garlic cloves * 12 oz (350g) drained can of tomatoes, chopped * 18 oz (540g) drained canned chick peas, reserve 8 fl oz (240 ml) of the liquid * 6 oz (180g) cooked macaroni * 3 Tablespoons chopped basil * Salt and pepper

Serves 4
Heat the oil in a saucepan over a medium heat. Add the onion and garlic and saute until the onion is translucent. Add the tomatoes and bring to the boil. Cover the saucepan, reduce the heat and simmer very gently for 5 minutes. Stir in the chick peas, the reserved liquid, macaroni, chopped basil, and a good sprinkling of salt and pepper. Stir until heated through. Serve garnished with a sprig of basil.

REGAL HAM CHICKEN SOUP

4 oz (100g) Smoked ham * 1 Cooked breast of chicken * 3 Hard boiled eggs * 1 Wine glass sherry * 3 Pints (1.75 Ltrs) stock * Salt and pepper

Serves 4
Chop up the chicken and ham very fine and also the hard boiled egg, put into a warmed soup tureen, pour the hot stock and sherry over and serve with croutons.

SAILOR'S SOUP

*2 lb (1 kg) Fish including heads and tails of some shellfish * Bay leaf * Peppercorns * Parsley * 2 Pts (1.15 litres) water * 2 Tablespoons white wine * 1 Small onion, chopped * 1 Stalk celery, chopped * 4 Tomatoes, peeled and chopped * 1 oz (25g) Butter * Salt and pepper*

Serves 4

Chop fish into pieces. Make stock by combining heads, skins and a couple of pieces of the cheaper fish with bay leaf, peppercorns, parsley and water. Boil for about 20 minutes. Meanwhile melt the butter in a saucepan and saute onion until golden brown, add celery, tomatoes, and seasoning. Saute a few minutes longer, add wine. Strain stock, bring to boil and gently poach remainder of fish until cooked. Combine with onion, tomatoes, celery and wine and serve with snippets of toast or fried bread.

It is suggested to make this soup into a particularly tasty and nourishing meal, try including with the fish, some sole, prawns or shrimps, a few scallops and a little smoked haddock or smoked cod fillet, just let your imagination work.

SOPA PARADISO

*4 Pts. (2.25 Ltr) Good soup stock * 4 Tablespoons breadcrumbs * Nutmeg * 4 Eggs, separated * 4 Tablespoons parmesan, grated * Salt and pepper*

Serves 6

Bring soup to the boil, slowly add the following mixture a spoonful at a time. Beat the egg whites till stiff, add beaten yolks and beat till well blended, then add cheese, breadcrumbs and seasoning. Boil 5-8 minutes and serve.

FISH

EEL FERRARA STYLE

*1 1/2lb (675 g) Eels, cleaned and cut into 1 inch (2.5 cm) slices *
*3 Tablespoons dry white wine * 1 Bay leaf * Little butter * Salt
and pepper * Pinch of mixed spice * Pinch of thyme * 1 Egg,
lightly beaten * Breadcrumbs*

Serves 4
Having prepared the eels, place in a casserole and over them pour the
wine mixed with the spices and herbs, add the bay leaf. Cover and
cook in a moderate oven for 45 minutes. At the end of that time lift
the eels from the sauce, drain and dip in oiled butter, then in the
beaten egg and breadcrumbs. Flavour if liked, with a little nutmeg, and
fry brown on both sides in hot butter.

MACKEREL WITH ROSEMARY AND GARLIC

*6 Tablespoons olive oil * 4 Cloves garlic * 4 Mackerel (about 9
3/4 lb 350g) each - cleaned but with heads and tails on
3 inch sprig fresh rosemary * Salt and pepper to taste * Juice of
1/2 lemon * Lemon wedges*

Serves 4
Wash the fish under cold running water and pat dry. Heat the oil in a
casserole and lightly saute the garlic. Add the fish and rosemary and
lower the heat to medium. Brown the fish well on each side but take
care it does not stick to the pan. When the fish is golden brown, add
lemon juice, cover with a tight fitting lid, turn the heat down to low,
and cook slowly for approximately 15 minutes until tender. Serve
piping hot with wedges of lemon.

RED MULLET FROM TRIESTE

*4 Medium size red mullet * Juice of 1/2 lemon * 3 Tablespoons
white wine * 1 Tablespoon olive oil * 1 Tablespoon chopped
capers*

Serves 4
Heat together in the pan the oil, lemon juice, capers and wine, and
after 10 minutes add the cleaned fish and allow to cook for 20 minutes,
turning the fish carefully at the end of half this time. Serve hot.

SWEET AND SOUR SARDINES

(Must be made day ahead)

*2 lb Fresh sardines * 2 Tablespoons raisins * Deep oil * 2
Onions, chopped * 2 Tablespoons wine vinegar * 1 Tablespoon
sugar * 2 Tablespoons pine nuts * 6 Sprigs parsley * Flour*

Serves 4
Soak raisins in warm water for 30 minutes. Clean sardines and wash
thoroughly in cold running water. Dry on paper towels. Coat sardines
with flour, shaking off excess. Deep fry sardines preferably in a basket,
chopped in preheated oil (360 degrees F) for 5-6 minutes. When they
are crisp and golden, drain on paper towelling. Meanwhile heat 3
tablespoons of oil in a pan and saute onions until translucent but not
brown. Stir in vinegar sugar, pine nuts, and drained raisins. Simmer
for a few minutes over low heat. Put sardines in shallow dish side by
side. Pour sauce over them. Sprinkle with parsley. Set dish aside and
let sardines marinate for 24 hours. Serve cold.

TUNA FROM LIGURIA

*1 lb (450g) Tunny, cut into thin slices * 2 anchovies * 1/2 oz
(15g) Dried mushrooms soaked in warm water for 10 minutes *
Salt and pepper * 1 Clove garlic, crushed * 1 Heaped tablespoon
chopped fresh parsley * 2 Tablespoons olive oil * 1/2 pt. (300 ml)
White wine * 1 Tablespoon flour * 1/2 Lemon * Butter*

Serves 4
Heat the oil, add the flour, then slowly add the wine, the anchovies
pounded to a paste and the other ingredients, except for the fish.
Allow to cook together for 10 minutes, stirring frequently. Add the
tunny fish and salt and pepper to taste. Cover the stewpan, and lower
the heat, allowing to cook slowly for 45 minutes. Remove the fish to a
hot dish, and to the sauce add a piece of butter the size of a walnut,
and the juice of a lemon. Bring this to boiling point and pour over the
fish. Serve hot.

SCAMPI FROM LOMBARDY

*36-40 Scampi or Dublin Bay prawns * 3 Tablespoons white wine vinegar * 1 Bay leaf * 1 Clove garlic, crushed * 4 Cloves * 1/2 small onion, chopped * 1 Tablespoon chopped parsley * A little chopped fennel * Salt to taste*

Serves 4

Mix together all the ingredients except the fish, and cook for 5 minutes in a stewpan. Then add the fish, removed from the shell, cover and cook over a medium heat for 15-20 minutes, stirring from time to time. Serve very hot.

VEAL 'BUNDLES' WITH ANCHOVIES AND CHEESE

*2 1/2 oz (60g) Butter * 10 Medium flat anchovy fillets * 1/2 oz (15g) Chopped parsley * 6 Tinned Italian tomatoes drained and seeds removed * Freshly ground pepper * 1 1/2 lb (680g) Veal escallops very thinly sliced & pounded flat * Salt * 8 oz (220g) Mozzarella cut into slices 1/2 inch (1cm) thick, or coarsely grated 2 oz (60g) Plain flour spread on a dish or on waxed paper * 1/2 Pint (275ml) dry marsala*

Serves 6

Put 1 oz (25g) of the butter and all the anchovies in a very small saucepan, and, over very low heat mash the anchovies to a pulp with a fork. Add the chopped parsley, the tomatoes and the pepper, turn the heat up to medium and cook stirring frequently, until the tomato thickens into sauce. Lay the escallops flat, sprinkle them with salt, spread the sauce over them, and cover except for 1/4 inch (6mm) edge all round, with a layer of cheese. Roll up the escallops, push the ends in and truss lightly, running the string both around the rolls and over the ends. In a frying pan that you can later hold all the bundles without crowding, melt the remaining butter over medium-high heat. When the butter foam begins to subside, roll the escallops lightly in the flour, shaking off the excess, and slide them into the frying pan. Brown on all sides for about 2 minutes. When the meat is well browned, add the marsala and turn the heat up high. While the wine boils, turn the rolls, and scrap up any browning residue in the pan. Cook for 2-3 minutes, stirring constantly, until the wine and cooking juices have turned into a creamy sauce. Transfer the meat and sauce to a warm dish and serve immediately.

MEAT AND POULTRY

CHICKEN BREASTS LOMBARDY STYLE

*2 Chicken Breasts * 1 Small onion * 1 Tablespoon Chopped Fennel * 1 or 2 Chicken Livers * 1 oz/25g Butter * 1 Teaspoon Chopped Parsley * 1 lb/450g Shelled Green Peas * 1/2 pt/300 ml Hot Stock or Water * Juice 1/2 Lemon * 2 Egg Yolks * Salt & Pepper*

Heat the butter in a stewpot and in it brown the chopped onion & parsley. Add the chicken, lightly floured, and brown on all sides, add the chopped fennel and the hot stock. Cover and allow to cook for 25 minutes. Meanwhile cook the peas in boiling salted water for 10 minutes, drain and add to the stewpan together with the chicken livers and seasoning. Cook for a further 10 minutes, then remove from the stove and stir in beaten egg yolks mixed with lemon juice.
Serve immediately.

GUINEA FOWL WITH SPICY SAUCE

*1 Guinea fowl 3 lbs (1300g) * Salt and pepper * Sage * 1 Clove garlic * 6 Tablespoons olive oil * Butter 3 oz (75g) * 1 Glass dry white wine*
***Spicy Sauce:** Chicken livers 3 oz (75g) * 2 Slices soft salami * 3 Anchovy fillets * 1 Clove garlic * Pickled green peppers 3 oz * 1/2 glass olive oil * Chopped parsley * Little clear stock * Juice of a lemon * Dash of wine vinegar*

Season the inside of the bird with salt, pepper and sage and a little garlic, then truss the bird. Put into a pan with oil, spread butter over the breast and put it into a hot oven. During cooking sprinkle the white wine over it, then baste with its own gravy. Remove all traces of gall from the chicken livers. Chop livers, the soft salami, anchovy fillets, garlic and pickled peppers. Fry all these ingredients lightly in the olive oil, adding chopped parsley and salt and pepper to taste. Add a little clear stock to the sauce during cooking. Pour it hot into a sauce boat, then add the juice of a lemon and a dash of wine vinegar. Quarter the Guinea fowl arranging it on the serving dish so that it appears whole. Serve with sauce.

HUNTER'S RABBIT

1 Rabbit 3 lbs (1350g) * *Peeled tomatoes 1 1/2 lb (700g)* *
Mushrooms 14 oz (400g) * *Olive Oil 1/2 glass* * *Butter 3 oz (75g)*
* *1 Onion, chopped* * *2 Tablespoons flour* * *1/2 Pint dry white*
wine * *Salt and pepper* * *1 Ladleful clear stock* * *Boiled*
potatoes

Serves 6
Cut rabbit into pieces. Strain tomatoes, and skin them and remove
seeds. Dip mushrooms quickly in water, dry and slice finely. Heat the
oil and butter in a pan. Fry the chopped onion, then add the pieces of
rabbit. When they have become golden brown sprinkle them with
flour. Stir the mixture well, then add the white wine, as soon as the
wine has evaporated, cover the rabbit with the tomatoes. Add the
mushrooms and when the mixture comes to the boil, season with salt
and pepper, cover the saucepan, lower the heat and cook slowly.
If the sauce becomes too thick, add a ladleful of clear stock.
Boil some potatoes, then cook them for a few minutes in the rabbit
sauce. Serve very hot.

ITALIAN BRAISED BEEF

1 Level tablespoon lard * *1 Tablespoon olive oil* * *1/2 lb (225g)*
Fat salt pork, diced * *1 onion sliced* * *2 Cloves garlic, chopped* *
2 1/2 lb (1.1kg) Lean beef, cut into like sized pieces * *Salt and*
black pepper * *1 Generous pinch marjoram* * *1/4 Pt Dry red wine*
* *4 Level-tablespoons tomato puree, diluted with water*

Serves 4-6
Combine lard and olive oil in a thick pan or flameproof casserole.
When fat begins to bubble add diced salt pork, sliced onion and
chopped garlic and saute until golden. Add pieces of meat seasoned
with salt and black pepper and marjoram and cook, stirring frequently
until meat is well browned on all sides. Now add dry red wine (one of
the rougher Italian ones), and continue cooking until the wine has been
reduced to half the original quantity. Add diluted tomato puree and
enough boiling water to cover the meat. Cover the pan and simmer
gently over a very low heat for about 2 hours, or until the meat is
tender and the savoury sauce is thick and richly coloured. A tablespoon
or two of red wine just before serving will add to the bouquet. Serve
direct from casserole.

NEAPOLITAN PORK CHOPS

*6 Pork chops * 2 Red or yellow peppers * 1 Tablespoon tomato paste * 8 oz (225g) Mushrooms * Oil for cooking * Salt and pepper * 1 Clove garlic crushed*

Serves 6

Heat the oil in a heavy frying pan. Fry garlic in it until it is pale brown, add the chops and brown on both sides. Add salt and pepper. Remove from the pan and keep warm. Meanwhile dilute the tomato paste with a little water and add to the pan in which the chops have been cooked, remove the seeds from the pepper and chop them finely, and add these to the pan together with the chopped mushrooms. Cover and cook slowly for about 15 minutes, then replace the chops, cooking together for another 20 minutes. Serve very hot.

PHEASANT COOKED IN MADEIRA

*1 Pheasant * 4 Rashes fat bacon * 2 Slices ham * 1/2 onion * 1 Stick celery * 1 Teaspoon chopped parsley * 1 Carrot * 2 oz (50g) Butter * Salt and pepper * Pinch of nutmeg * 1/4 Pt. (150 ml) Madeira * Fried bread*

Serves 4

Melt butter in a stewpan and put in pheasants with bacon, ham and onion cut small, finely chopped celery, parsley, diced carrot, salt, pepper and nutmeg. Cook together slowly until the pheasant begins to brown then add the madeira and stock. Cover the stewpan and allow about 45 minutes for the bird to finish cooking. Then place the pheasant in a hot dish, strain the fat from the sauce, pass through a sieve and pour over the bird. Serve garnished with croutons of fried bread.

STUFFED STEAK

*Approx 2 lb (1 kg) Veal steak cut into thin layers and flattened with a palette * 2 oz (50g) Lean ham * 2 Cloves garlic crushed * 1 Teaspoon chopped parsley * 2 oz (50g) Grated parmesan cheese * 2 Slices of bread, soaked in milk or water, squeezed dry * 1 Egg yolk * Pinch of nutmeg * Salt and pepper * Onion * 1 Stalk celery * 1 Carrot*

Serves 4

Chop the ham in small pieces and to it add the other ingredients and mix well. Cut the steak into strips 7 inches (18 cm) in length and 3 inches (7.5cm) wide, and on each spread a portion of the filling. Roll the steak round the filling and fasten with a thread. In a heavy pan heat 2 oz (50g) butter and, if available, a little marrow from a bone, and in this place the rolls of steak and allow to brown on all sides. Add a chopped carrot and stalk of celery cut small. Cover the pan and allow to cook together for 20 minutes adding, towards the end of the cooking time, a few tablespoons of good stock or strained tomato sauce.

DESSERTS

ALMOND PASTRY LIGURIAN STYLE

Makes 1 8 inch square pan

Time 1 1/2 hours, oven temp, 350 F

*3/4 Cup blended almonds * 6 Tablespoons butter * 1 Cup sugar*
*1/2 Cup sifted flour * 3 Tablespoons brandy * Icing sugar*

Roast almonds in a frying pan over low heat until richly browned.
Chop very fine. Melt butter, stir in sugar and eggs, gradually stir in
flour, almonds and brandy. Butter and flour on 8 inch square pan.
Pour batter into it and bake in a preheated oven for 20-25 minutes or
until lightly browned. Let it cool in pan. Cut into small squares.
Arrange on a serving platter and sprinkle with icing sugar.

ITALIAN STUFFED PEACHES

*4 Medium peaches * 2 Tablespoons butter * 1 Tablespoon caster*
*sugar * 1 Tablespoon desiccated coconut * 2 Teaspoons cocoa **
*1 Egg beaten * 1/2 Teaspoon almond flavour * 4 digestive*
*biscuits, crushed * 3 Tablespoons marsala wine*

Serves 4
Preheat the oven to 375 F, Gas mark 6. Cut the peaches in half and
remove the stones. Scoop out some of the flesh from each peach with
a teaspoon, leaving a sufficient border to retain the shape of the fruit.
Chop the peach flesh and put onto one side. In a small bowl mix
together 4 teaspoons of butter with the sugar. When well blended stir
in the coconut and cocoa. Stir in the egg, almond flavouring, digestive
crumbs and reserved peach flesh, mix well. Arrange the peaches, cut
side up, in an ovenproof dish just large enough to hold the halves.
Divide the stuffing evenly between the peach halves. Pour the wine
into the dish and dot the remaining butter around the peaches and in
the wine. Bake in the preheated oven for 20-25 minutes until the
peaches are beginning to brown. Serve warm or chilled with the juices
from the dish poured over the peach halves.

BRANDIED MERINGUES

*2 Egg whites * 1 Cup icing sugar * 1 Tablespoon brandy * 1 1/2 Tablespoons butter * 2 Tablespoons flour * Oven temp 250 deg F*

Makes 20
Warm egg whites to room temperature. Beat egg whites until stiff. Gradually beat in icing sugar, 2 tablespoons at a time, until stiff and glossy. Fold in brandy. Put mixture in a pastry bag with a 3/4 inch diameter round opening. Force out 3 inch lengths onto a heavily buttered and floured baking sheet, 2 inches apart to allow for spreading. Bake in a preheated oven until they are hard - about 40 minutes. Let cool on baking sheet. Remove carefully from baking sheet and arrange on a serving platter.

ITALIAN FRUIT CAKE WITH PLUM

Makes 9 inch square cake * Time 1-1 1/2 hours

Soak fruit 2-3 hours * Oven Temp 350 degrees F.

*1/2 Cup chopped dry figs * 1/2 Cup chopped dates * 1/2 Cup raisins * 1/2 Cup rum * 1 - 3/4 Cups all purpose flour * 2 Tsp. baking powder * 1/2 Cup butter * 2-3 Cups milk * 1 Tsp. vanilla * 2 Eggs*

Marinate fruit in rum for 2-3 hours, stirring from time to time. Sift flour and baking powder. Cream butter until fluffy in a mixing bowl. Gradually beat in sugar. Beat in eggs and milk alternately beginning and ending with flour. Stir in vanilla. Drain rum from fruit. Fold fruit into cake batter. Pour mixture into a greased and floured 9" square pan. Bake in a preheated oven for about 40-45 minutes until firm to the touch in the centre. Cool in pan and then cut into squares to serve.

CHOCOLATE MOCHA PUDDING

*3 Egg yolks * 1/2 Cup caster sugar * 8 oz (squares) semi-sweet chocolate * 3/4 Cup butter * 1 Tablespoon instant coffee * 1 Cup sweetened whipped cream * 4 Coffee beans * 2 Tablespoons chopped pistachio nuts*

Serves 4

Beat egg yolks with 5 tablespoons of the sugar, heating mixture with a whisk until creamy. Grate chocolate into a saucepan. Melt over hot water. Let cool, mix butter with remaining sugar in a separate bowl until soft and creamy. Stir in egg mixture, instant coffee and melted chocolate. Fold in whipped cream a little at a time. Pour the mixture into a 3 cup pudding mold and refrigerate for 3-4 hours. Shortly before serving dip mold into luke warm water for a moment, placing the pudding onto a dressing platter. Garnish with coffee beans and chopped pistachio nuts.

MONT BLANC

*1 lb (450g) Italian chestnuts * 1/4 Pt. (150ml) Double cream * 8 oz (225g) Caster sugar * Salt*

Serves 4

Cut a slit in the chestnuts at the pointed end and place them a dozen at a time in a very hot oven for 10 minutes, after which they will peel easily. When all are peeled, place in boiling water and allow to simmer for an hour or until they are tender. Strain and mash the nuts, adding the sugar and a pinch of salt. Pull them through a potato sieve allowing them to pile up in a pyramid form on a dish. The less you touch them the better, otherwise the light appearance of the finished dish is apt to be spoiled. Whip the cream, flavouring it if you like with a little good liquor, and pile it lightly on top of the mound of chestnuts, rather like snow on a mountain top.

SICILIAN CAKE

*1 lb (450g) Ricotta cheese * 14 oz (450g) Icing sugar * 1/2 Small glass orange flower water * 3 oz (75g) Candied pumpkin * 3 oz (75g) Candied orange * 2 oz (50g) Chocolate broken into pieces * 12 slices sponge cake * 1 Candied orange * 3 oz (75g) Green glace cherries * 3 oz (75g) Red glace cherries*

Serves 6
Sieve the ricotta into a bowl and flavour it with icing sugar and orange flower water. Mix well with wooden spoon until the ricotta is thick, like whipped cream. Add some cubes of candied fruit and the chocolate pieces. Line a shallow tin with greaseproof paper. Cover the bottom with slices of sponge cake and spread some creamed ricotta over them. Cover the ricotta with more slices of sponge cake and put it into the refrigerator for a few hours. Spread a thin layer of the ricotta cream over the top and decorate the cake. Put a candied orange in the centre, place slices of candied pumpkin around the orange and put green and red glace cherries around the edge of the cake.

SWEET FRITTERS

*2 Egg yolks * 1 Pint (600ml) cream * 2 Tablespoons sugar * 2 oz (50g) flour * A little chopped candied citron * Breadcrumbs*

Serves 4
Beat together the egg yolks until well mixed, blend in the flour and peach in a double boiler cooking until thick and being careful not to allow it to boil, otherwise the yolks will curdle. If the cream does not seem to be thick enough, a little semolina may be added towards the end of the cooking time. Stir in the citron.
Pour on a flat plate that has been lightly oiled or greased with butter. Allow to cool, cut into pieces 2 inches (5 cm) square; dip in white of egg and then in breadcrumbs. Fry in butter until golden brown. Serve hot, sprinkled with sugar.

ZABAGLIONE

This dish must not be cooked over direct heat. It is necessary to have a double boiler. Since it is desirable for the upper part to have a heavy bottom, you might use an enamelled cast iron saucepan or other heavy pot and hold it over water simmering in any other kind of pot. Be sure to choose a large enough pot - the mixture increases greatly in volume as you heat.

*4 Egg yolks * Granulated sugar 3/4 oz (50g) * 8 Tablespoons Marsala*

Serves 6

Put the yolks and the sugar in the heavy bottomed pot and mix in an electric blender until they are pale golden and creamy. In a slightly larger second pot bring water to the brink of a simmer, not to the boil. Place the pot with the whipped yolks over the second pot. Add the marsala and continue heating. The mixture which will begin to foam, and then swell into a light, soft mass, is ready when it forms soft mounds. Spoon it into goblets, and serve immediately.

SAUCES

BOLOGNESE SAUCE

*3 Tablespoons olive oil * 1 oz (25 g) Butter * 4 oz (120g)
Unsmoked streaky bacon, rinded and diced * 1 Small onion, very
finely chopped * 1 Small carrot very finely chopped * 1 Stalk
celery, very finely chopped * 1 Clove garlic, peeled and crushed *
2 oz (50g) Chicken livers trimmed and chopped * 4 Fl oz (110 ml)
Dry white wine * 12 oz (340g) Best minced beef * 2 Tablespoons
tomato puree * 4 Fl oz (110 ml) Beef stock * Salt and freshly
ground black pepper * 4 Tablespoons single cream*

Serves 4
Put the oil, butter, bacon, onion, carrot and celery into a heavy
saucepan and cook over a moderate heat, stirring from time to time,
until the vegetables are soft. Add the garlic, beef and chicken livers and
saute until the beef has lost its pinkness. Pour in the wine and boil
briskly until reduced by more than half. Mix the tomato puree with the
stock and add to the pan. Check the seasoning and bring to the boil.
Mix well and simmer very gently, uncovered, for 2-2 1/2 hours, stirring
occasionally. The sauce should on no account boil, but just break into
an occasional bubble, if the sauce gets too dry, add a little warm water.
15 Minutes before it is ready, stir in the cream. Excellent with any
pasta, especially spaghetti.

MARINARA SAUCE

*1 Medium sized onion * 4 Tablespoons olive oil * 1/2 Pt. (300
ml) Dry white wine * 1 Pt. (600 ml) Shrimps * 1 Clove garlic,
crushed * 6 Tomatoes, peeled * 1/2 Teaspoon brown sugar *
Salt and pepper to taste*

Serves 4
Heat the oil in a heavy pan and in it cook the chopped onion and
crushed garlic until golden. Add tomatoes, cut small, together with
sugar and salt and pepper. Lower heat and allow to cook gently for 20
minutes. While this is cooking, peel and add shrimps, and add them
together with the wine to the tomato mixture cooking gently together
for 15 minutes. Serve hot over pasta of any type.

MUSHROOM AND TOMATO SAUCE

*1 lb (450g) Mushrooms * 1 Medium sized can tomatoes * 3 Tablespoons olive oil * 1 Clove garlic crushed * Cayenne pepper to taste * 1 Tablespoon chopped basil * Pinch chopped thyme * Pinch salt*

Serves 6

Heat oil and in it allow the crushed garlic to brown. Add mushrooms, sliced finely, and simmer for 10 minutes. Pass tomatoes through a sieve, and add to the sauce together with the remaining ingredients. Cover and allow to cook very slowly for an hour, stirring from time to time. Serve very hot as a sauce with any type of pasta.

NEAPOLITAN TOMATO SAUCE

*1 lb (450g) Tomatoes * 2 Stalks celery * Few leaves of fresh basil * 1 Onion * 1 Carrot * Salt and pepper to taste*

Serves 4

Wash tomatoes and cut in pieces and place in a saucepan with other vegetables cut coarsely. Allow to cook slowly for 30 minutes or until the vegetables are tender. Remove from heat and pass through a sieve. Season with salt and pepper. Add a knob of fresh lard at the end of cooking and mix well with the sauce, and just before serving a little freshly chopped basil makes an excellent finishing touch.

PIZZAIOLA SAUCE

*1 Tablespoon olive oil * 6 Good sized tomatoes * Salt and pepper * 3 Crushed garlic cloves * 1 Tablespoon fresh oregano*

Serves 4

Heat the oil and allow crushed garlic to cook gently in it. Add peel and cut up tomatoes, salt and pepper and cook fairly fast until the tomatoes are cooked through but not reduced to a pulp. Add a good tablespoon or oregano, and before serving add another clove of garlic cut very fine. An excellent sauce to serve with beefsteak.

5
Jewish Cuisine

The cookery of a people, like all other aspects of its culture, is a reflection of it's history and like the rest of the culture it does not develop overnight. It is therefore not surprising that Jewish cooking has developed characteristics of it's own which make it different from any other cookery. Probably in no other religious or ethnic tradition do diet and food have more importance.

The Jewish dietary laws (kashruth), which prohibit the use of certain food entirely and the mixing of other foods at the same meal, foster the imaginative use of available foods. It is such inventiveness that creates great artistry in cooking.

Jews have for many centuries been influenced by biblical prohibitions and within these restrictions, the art of food preparation was developed and expanded. In time certain dishes became associated with specific holidays and festivals in addition to the sabbath.

The true gourmet has become very interested in the international flavour of Jewish cooking. The dishes of many lands were adopted and varied by Jewish cooks over the years due to the fact that for almost 2000 years they were without a homeland and they were compelled to make the most of whatever food was available to them. At the same time they have always been confined by dietary commandments and rituals which are still observed by many today.

The rules of the kashruth do not in any way limit the variety of dishes. They merely ensure that food is completely fresh.

Since Israel became an independent state it has developed it's own native cuisine. Each influx of immigrants tends to retain its ethnic cookery, but in every day life Israelis eat simply - their meals are based on raw vegetables (particularly cucumbers and avocado pears), dairy produce, and citrus fruits.

Like their Middle Eastern neighbours, they are fond of vegetable purees, spiced meatballs etc. Israeli farmers rear large numbers of turkeys and ducks. In the latter they have developed a new breed. It is a point of interest that even the shape of some foods relate to biblical characters, like the 'Ears of Harman', a cake served at the feast of Purim. Fasts, (at least three of 24 hours duration during the year), are the excuse for some splendid feasts before and after. Although Jewish religious precepts forbid greed and drunkenness, they do not forbid good eating.

Perhaps because of dark memories of ghetto and near starvation, Jews are generous and hospitable beyond the ordinary. While they like and appreciate the best of the dishes in 'haute cuisine' (which do not infringe on their religious observances), they have, and always will have, a sentimental and nostalgic attachment to home cooking made the way 'mama used to make them'.

Starters

Starters are a relatively new aspect of Jewish cookery which has now adopted and adapted these from all over the world. They have become very much an integral part of a Jewish meal. Fish cocktails, fruit cups, small salads, and clear soups as well as large canapes are served at the table as a first course. The selected recipes include flavours very much enjoyed by Jewish people, and with the application of a little imagination, a delectable array of these dainties can be created. A beautiful tray of appetisers makes a most exciting display of colour and flavours that are pleasing to the eye, and of course, a great pleasure to eat.

STARTERS

EGGS STUFFED WITH MUSHROOMS

*4 Large eggs * 1 Tablespoon onion, chopped * Olive oil for frying * 1/4 lb (125g) Small button mushrooms, sliced * Salt and pepper * Dash of sugar * 1/2 Teaspoon tomato puree * Tablespoon single cream * Teaspoon water*

Serves 4
Hard boil the eggs, slice them in half lengthwise, and mash the yolks. Saute the chopped onion in a little oil, add the mushrooms reserving a few slices for decoration. Season with salt and pepper, and sugar and add the tomato puree. Chop the mushroom mixture and mix with the egg yolks. Stir in the cream, and pile the mixture into the cooked egg whites. Garnish with sliced mushrooms.

HERRING AND SOUR CREAM SALAD

*4 Pickled Herrings * 1 Small onion * 1 Crisp eating apple, brushed with lemon juice * 1/4 Pt. (150 ml) Sour cream*

Serves 4
Drain herrings well and cut into wide strips. Arrange on a serving dish. Slice the onion and blend for one minute in boiling water. Slice the apple. Mix the herring with the apple and onion and cover with the sour cream. Serve chilled with wholemeal bread.

PINK GRAPEFRUIT COCKTAIL

*2 Large pink grapefruit * 2 Small oranges * 4 oz (125g) Large white grapes * Sugar to taste * Chinese gooseberry*

Serves 4
Make small diagonal cuts around the centre of the grapefruit and continue cutting until the two halves can be separated. Remove the flesh of the fruit with a grapefruit knife and then cut between the membranes to remove the segments. Place these together with the juice, into a bowl. Peel the oranges and also remove the segments from these, being careful to avoid the pith and membranes. Add the orange pieces to the grapefruit with the pipped grapes and add sugar to taste. Spoon all the fruit mixture the juices back into the grapefruit shells and top each one with a slice of Chinese gooseberry. Chill well.

POTATOES STUFFED WITH MEAT

*1 lb (450 g) Beef minced * 1 Slice white bread, soaked in water and drained * 2 Eggs * 1 Tablespoon parsley chopped * 1 Small onion, chopped * 5 Large potatoes, peeled * 6 Cloves garlic * 1/2 Teaspoon black pepper * 1/4 Teaspoon saffron * Oil for frying * Water * Salt*

Serves 5

Mix the meat well with bread, onion, parsley, egg and salt. Set aside cut potatoes in two, lengthwise. Scoop out the middle part of each half, and set aside. Stuff the hollowed potatoes with meat mixture, coat in flour, then dip in beaten egg, and fry in oil until golden. After frying is completed, pour remainder of frying oil into a saucepan. In it, saute garlic. Add scooped out portions of potatoes. On top arrange the fried stuffed potatoes, season with salt, pepper and saffron, and put in water to cover. Cook over high heat until boiling point is reached, reduce heat and continue to cook over low heat until potatoes are cooked. Serve with pickles.

STUFFED COURGETTES IN LEMON SAUCE

*1 lb (450g) Courgettes, halved * 6 Tablespoons oil for frying * 1 Small onion, chopped * 1 oz (25 g) Rice * 2 oz (50 g) Pine nuts * Pinch of oregano * 1 Clove garlic, minced * Salt and pepper * 1/2 Pt (1/4 ltr) Chicken stock*
***SAUCE:** 2 Egg yolks * Juice of 1/2 Lemon * 3 Fl oz (75 ml) Chicken stock*

Preheat the oven to 350 degrees F, 180 degrees C, Gas Mark 4. Scoop the centres out of the halved courgettes and saute the halves in oil for a few minutes. Remove them to a greased ovenproof dish. For the filling, saute the onion and chopped courgettes until they are golden, add the rice, pine nuts, oregano and seasoning, and then cover with hot chicken stock. Simmer for about 10 minutes until the rice is tender, and then fill the courgettes with the mixture. Bake, covered for about 40 minutes. After about 30 minutes prepare the sauce. Beat the egg yolks with the lemon juice in a bowl. Pour on the hot stock, season, and in a pan, over a low heat, stir gently until the sauce thickens slightly. Do not boil, and as soon as it is thick, remove it from the heat and serve with the stuffed courgettes.

TOMATOES IN CREAM DRESSING

*2 Teaspoons oil * Juice of 1/2 Lemon * Salt and pepper * 1/2 Clove garlic * 4 Large tomatoes, peeled * 1 Tablespoon chives and parsley chopped * 2 Tablespoons whipped cream.*

Mix the oil, lemon juice, salt and pepper in a screw top jar and shake well. Add a cut piece of garlic clove and leave to allow the taste to infuse while you prepare the tomatoes. Slice the tomatoes thinly and arrange them in a bowl. Pour a few spoonfuls of the dressing over the tomatoes and then cover with the whipped cream. Sprinkle with the chopped herbs and refrigerate for a while before serving.

TAHINA (Sesame paste or cocktail dip)

*5 1/4 oz Sesame seeds * 1/2 Pt. Water * 2 Cloves garlic * Juice of 2 lemons * 1 Teaspoon salt * Pinch of cayenne*
To Garnish: *3 Tablespoons olive oil * 3 Tablespoons chopped parsley * Sprinkling of paprika * Olives*

Put the sesame seeds, water, garlic and lemon juice through a blender to make a paste. Add more water if needed, to achieve mayonnaise like consistency. Add the seasoning. Serve flattened on little plates garnished with a swirl of olive oil, sprinkling of parsley and paprika and centred with olives.

SOUPS

CHERRY WINE SOUP

*1 lb (450g) Red cherries * 3 Cloves * 1 Small stick of cinnamon * 7 oz (225g) Sugar * 2 Pts. (1200 ml) * 3 Tablespoons cornflour * 1/2 Pt. (300 ml) Red table wine * 1/2 Teaspoon grated lemon rind * Lemon juice to taste * Sour cream for garnish*

Serves 6
Cook the cherries, cloves, cinnamon, sugar and water until the cherries are tender. Remove the spices. Dissolve the spices. Dissolve the cornflour in the wine, add the lemon rind and juice and stir into the cherry liquid. Cook until clear. Serve chilled with a topping of sour cream.

BUTTER BEAN SOUP

*8 oz (225g) Carrots, chopped * 10 oz (275g) Onions, chopped * 1 Tablespoon margarine * 1 lb (450g) Butterbeans, previously soaked * 1 Pt. (1/2 ltr) Meat stock (beef or lamb) * Salt and pepper*

Serves 4
Saute the chopped vegetables in the fat, turning well to coat, and then cook for about 10 minutes until they start to soften. Add the drained, soaked beans and pour on the meat stock. Then simmer for 4-5 hours until the beans are tender. Put the soup through a sieve, or blend until smooth. Add a little more soup stock or water to make up to about 2 pints (1 ltr) and season to taste. Serve very hot with croutons or crisp bread rolls.

ONION SOUP WITH PORT

*1 Knuckle of Veal * 2 Pts. (1 ltr) Water * 3 Tablespoons oil * 1 1/2 lb (3/4 kg) onions, sliced thinly * 4 oz (115 g) Mushrooms * 1/4 Pt. (150 ml) White wine * Salt * Pepper * Bouquet garni * 4 Eggs * 4 Liquor glasses port*

Make veal stock by cooking knuckle in water for 2 hours. Strain. Heat oil in a heavy casserole. Fry sliced onions and mushrooms until golden. Cover onions and mushrooms with stock and white wine. Season with salt and pepper, and add bouquet garni. Cover with lid and place in a cool oven 300 degrees F, 150 degrees C, gas 2 for 2 hours. Remove from oven and rub through a sieve. When ready to serve, whisk together 4 eggs and port in a soup tureen. Pour on the soup, swirl tureen gently and serve.

FRESH PEA SOUP WITH MINT

*1/2 Onion, chopped * Stick celery chopped * 1/2 oz (40 g) Butter * 1 lb (450 g) Fresh peas (after shelling) * 1 Bunch fresh mint * 1 Pt. (1/2 ltr) Water * 1/2 Pt. (1/4 ltr) Milk*

Saute the onion and celery in the butter until they are a light golden colour. Add the shelled peas and several leaves of mint, then pour on the water, season well and simmer until the vegetables are tender. Remove the mint leaves and sieve or blend the mixture to make a puree. Heat the milk and add this to the puree, stirring well. Taste for seasoning. Serve very hot in individual bowls, garnish with a swirl of cream and chopped mint and parsley.

POTATO SOUP

*3 Large carrots * 2 Leeks * 1 Onion * 2 Stalks celery * 1 oz (25 g) Butter * 3 Medium potatoes * 1/2 Pt. (1/4 ltr) Creamy milk * Salt and pepper*

Make a vegetable stock with 1 1/2 carrots, 1 1/2 leeks, 1/2 onion, and the celery. Place them all in a pan and cover with water. Bring to the boil and simmer for about 1 hour. Meanwhile shred the remaining onion, leek and carrot into julienne strips and saute them in butter. Cook the potatoes in a little salted water and drain them. Put the potatoes, milk and stock into a blender until the mixture is a smooth puree. Add the vegetable strips. Re-heat gently, adjust seasoning and serve hot.

TOMATO RICE SOUP

*3/4 Pt (425 ml) Tomato pulp (fresh or tinned tomatoes, sieved) * 1/2 Teaspoon celery salt * 2 pts. (1 Ltr) Beef stock * 2 Pts. (1 Ltr) Water * 1/2 Teaspoon sugar * Salt and pepper * 1 oz (25g) Rice*

Serves 4
Put all the ingredients except the rice into a saucepan and bring to the boil. Simmer for about 30 minutes, then add the rice. Continue boiling gently for about 10 minutes when the rice will be cooked and the soup will be a dark rich colour. Taste for seasoning and serve hot.

FISH

The fish course is a very important element in Jewish cookery, fishermen still cast their nets in the Sea of Galilee which is really a lake, as they have done for thousands of years and fishing boats go far out to sea. Carp is one of the most popular fish dishes and the Israelis have their own specialities such as St. Peter's fish (recipe below) from Lake Gennosanet, and fish which is dressed in their much loved Tahina (recipe page 99).

BARBECUED ST. PETER'S FISH

*12 x 8 inch St. Peter's fish or trout * Oil * 4 Onions cut into thick slices * Parsley sprigs * Salt and pepper * Lemon juice * Cayenne*

Serves 6
Oil the rack over barbecue grill. Brush the fish inside and out with oil, and sprinkle with salt, cayenne pepper, and put a slice of onion and a sprig of parsley in the cavity of each fish. Grill over embers, browning well before turning. Sprinkle on lemon juice and oil during grilling. Cook for about 15 minutes or until fish are done.

CARP IN PAPRIKA

*4 lb (2 kg) Fresh carp * 4 Sweet fleshy green peppers * 1 lb (450g) Fresh tomatoes * 1 1/2 Teaspoons salt * 5 oz (140 g) Finely chopped onions * 4 oz (115 g) Margarine * 1 1/2 Teaspoons paprika * 4 Tablespoons water * Salt*

Serves 8
Chop the peppers and the tomatoes. Cut the carp into serving pieces. Sprinkle the fish with salt. Lightly fry the finely chopped onions in the margarine, stirring often. Sprinkle with the paprika and add the water. Cook until the onions become mushy. Add the chopped green peppers and the chopped tomatoes and bring to the boil. Place the fish in a baking dish and pour on the paprika sauce. Bake for about 45 minutes in a moderate oven 350 degrees F, Gas 4, basting from time to time.

HALIBUT WITH WINE AND CHEESE SAUCE

*4 Steaks * Salt and pepper * 8 1/2 Fl oz (250 ml) Dry white wine
* 6 Tablespoons thick bechamel sauce * 4 Heaped tablespoons
grated tasty cheese*

Serves 4

Place the fish in a greased ovenproof dish, season carefully and cover
with the wine. Cook in a preheated oven at 350 degrees F, 180
degrees C, Gas 4, for about 10 minutes, then pour the wine into a
small saucepan, leaving the fish in the oven dish. Bring the wine to the
boil, reduce it to about half its original quantity and then stir in the
bechamel sauce. Pour the wine mixture over the fish and sprinkle over
the grated cheese. Return to the oven for a further 10 minutes, and
serve when the cheese sauce is bubbling.

LEMON SOLE WITH SPINACH

*6 Fillets lemon sole * 1/2 Pt. (1/4 Ltr) Dry white wine * 1 lb (450
g) Fresh spinach * Salt and pepper * 2 oz (50 g) Butter * 2 oz
(50 g) Flour * 1/2 Pt. (1/4 Ltr) Single Cream * 3 oz (75 g) Grated
cheese*

Serves 6

Place the rolled up fish fillets in a shallow pan and cover with the wine.
Simmer gently for about 10 minutes until the fish is opaque. Cook the
spinach for about 10 minutes over a low heat, without adding any extra
water. Drain, and season well and chop it roughly. Butter a fairly
shallow ovenproof dish and place the cooked spinach on the base, then
carefully lay the drained fillets on the top. Make a bechamel sauce with
the butter, flour and cream and add some of the strained juice from the
fish, stirring all the time. Pour the sauce over the fish and add the
grated cheese. Place it under a hot grill for a few minutes to brown the
top. Serve at once.

SHERRY SOLE AU GRATIN

*2 Large sole, filleted * 2 oz (50g) Butter * 1 Large onion, chopped finely * 1/2 Pt. (285 ml) Tomato puree * 3 Tablespoons dry sherry * 1 Teaspoon salt * Dash of pepper * 1/4 Pt. (140 ml) Single cream * 4 oz (115 g) Grated cheddar cheese * Parsley*

Serves 2

Fry fillets and place them in an ovenproof dish. Heat butter and saute chopped onion. When golden add the tomato puree, sherry, salt, pepper and cream. Stir and bring to the boil. Pour over the fillets. Top with the grated cheese and bake in a fairly hot oven, 400 degrees F, 200 degrees C, Gas 6 for about 30 minutes. Decorate with parsley and serve with creamed potatoes.

TROUT WITH ANCHOVY SAUCE

*6 Medium/large trout * Plain flour * 9 Tablespoons oil * 4 oz (115 g) Butter * 2 oz (50g) Tinned anchovy fillets, diced finely * 1 Tablespoon chopped parsley * 1 Tablespoon chopped spring onion * 1 Tablespoons chopped blanched almonds * Dash of oregano * Pinch black pepper * 1 Tablespoon lemon juice * 1/4 Pt. (140 ml) Dry white wine * 1 Tablespoon dry sherry*

Serves 6

Coat the trout in flour. Heat oil and fry trout for about 2 minutes. Remove to a hot serving platter. Melt butter in a pan, and add anchovies, parsley, spring onion, almonds, oregano, black pepper, and lemon juice. Pour over wine and sherry. Simmer for a few minutes. Pour sauce over trout. Serve immediately.

MEAT AND POULTRY

BEEF AND BUTTER BEANS

*1 1/2 lb (680 g) Chuck steak * 1/2 lb (250 g) Butter beans * 2
Onions * 1 Tablespoon margarine * 1 Pt. (1/2 ltr) Water * Salt
and pepper * 1 Pt. (1/2 ltr) Water*

Serves 4
Soak the butter beans overnight in cold water. Slice the onions and
saute them in the margarine. Transfer them to a casserole and then
saute the meat until it is brown on each side. Add it, with the drained
beans, to the onions in the casserole. Stir the pan juices with the hot
water and pour this over the meat, onions and beans. Season well.
Cook at 350 degrees F, 180 degrees C, Gas mark 4, for about 3
hours, checking halfway through the cooking time to see that there is
enough liquid.

CHICKEN SOUFFLE

*3 Egg yolks * 8 oz (225 g) Cooked breast of chicken, minced, with
salt, pepper, and paprika * 5 Egg whites * 2 oz (50 g) Almonds,
blanched and flaked*
Chicken Sauce: *2 oz (50 g) Chicken fat or margarine * 2 oz (50
g) Flour * 8 Fl oz (225 ml) Chicken stock * Salt and pepper*

Serves 4
First make the chicken sauce. Melt the fat and add the flour, stirring
well. Gradually add the stock and continue stirring until the sauce
thickens. Add the seasoning and leave to cool slightly. Prepare an 8
inch (20 cm) souffle dish with a greased collar rising about 2 inches (5
cm) above the rim of the dish. Preheat the oven, 375 degrees F, 190
degrees C, gas 5. Add the egg yolks to the chicken sauce, and then
fold in the cooked minced chicken. Season with salt, pepper and a
little paprika. Make sure the whites are at room temperature and whisk
them until they are stiff, but not dry. Fold them into the chicken
mixture, being careful not to stir too much as this will prevent the
souffle from rising. As soon as the egg whites are incorporated, spoon
the mixture into the prepared dish and scatter the almonds on top.
Cook in the centre of the oven for 25 minutes without opening the
door. Serve immediately.

CHICKEN WITH WALNUTS AND GRAPES

*3 - 3 1/2 lb (1.6 kg) Chicken, cut into 8 portions * Salt and black pepper * 3 oz (75 g) Clear honey * 2 Tablespoons cooking oil * 1 oz (25 g) Vegetarian margarine * 4 oz (100 g) Broken walnuts * 4 oz (100 g) Seedless grapes*
***Garnish:** Walnut halves * Halved seedless grapes*

Season the chicken portions with salt and pepper, and brush with some of the honey. Heat the oil and margarine in a pan, and saute the chicken portions skin side down for about 8 minutes until golden. Turn and cook the other side for about 4 minutes until the meat is cooked through. Remove from the pan and keep warm. Add the remaining honey and the walnuts to the pan, and cook for about 4 minutes, then add the grapes, and cook for a further 2 minutes. Serve on a bed of rice, surrounded by walnuts and grapes.

SWEET AND SOUR POT ROAST

*4 lbs (2 1/4 kg) Beef * 2 Large onions, sliced * 1 Clove garlic, minced * 1/2 Cup of water * 2 Bay leaves * 6 Potatoes, quartered * 2 Tablespoons vinegar * 1 Tablespoon brown sugar * 3 Tablespoons ketchup * 1/2 Cup raisins*

Serves 8
Brown the meat on all sides in a heavy pan. Add and brown the onions and garlic. Add water and bay leaves. Cover and simmer for 1 hour. Add more hot water if needed. Add potatoes, vinegar and brown sugar. Cover and simmer for another hour. Add salt, ketchup and raisins. Cover and cook for a further 1/2 hour.

DESSERTS

In common with the rest of the Middle East, fresh fruit is frequently served for dessert. Milk puddings made from rice or ground rice are also very popular and are served with syrup or honey and a sprinkling of nuts.

CHERRY COMPOTE

*4 oz (100 g) Castor sugar * 1/2 Pt. (300 ml) Water * 1 Teaspoon arrowroot * 1 lb (450 g) White cherries * 1 Tablespoon rosewater * 2 Tablespoons warmed brandy*

Serves 4
Bring water to the boil with sugar and rosewater. Remove from heat. Mix the arrowroot with a little cold water and pour into the hot syrup, stirring all the time. Bring to the boil again, and stir until the arrowroot has become transparent, about 4 minutes. Put in the washed and stoned cherries and simmer for 5 minutes only. Remove from the heat and allow to cool in dish to be served at table. Serve slightly warm. Set the brandy alight and pour over at the last moment.

APPLES WITH CINNAMON

*6 Cooking apples * 3 Tablespoons soft brown sugar * 4 oz (100 g) Ratafia biscuits * 2 oz (50 g) Unsalted butter * 2 Tablespoons ground cinnamon * 2 Tablespoons water*

Serves 6
Peel and core and quarter the apples and place in a greased baking dish. Crumble the ratafias and sprinkle over them. Mix the sugar and cinnamon and spread on top. Dot with the butter and pour on the water. Bake in a moderate oven for 30 minutes and serve warm.

DRIED FRUIT SALAD

*4 oz (100 g) Dried apricots * 4 oz (100 g) Prunes * 4 oz (100 g) Dried figs * 2 oz (50 g) Seedless raisins * 2 Tablespoons rosewater * 2 oz (50 g) Slivers of almonds*

Serves 4
Soak the dried fruit overnight, then drain and place in a saucepan. Cover with boiling water, and simmer for 20-30 minutes until the fruit is tender. Stir in the rosewater, and serve hot or cold, sprinkled with nuts.

RICE PUDDING

*4 oz (100 g) Long grain rice * 1 3/4 Pt. (750 ml) Water * 1 Pt. (600 ml) Milk * 1 Tablespoon rosewater * Pinch of salt * 2 oz (50 g) Granulated sugar * Ground cinnamon*

Cook the rice uncovered in the water for 20-25 minutes until the water is absorbed. Add the milk, rosewater, salt and sugar, bring to the boil and simmer for 25 minutes. Pour into a serving dish, sprinkle with cinnamon, and leave to cool. Serve with honey,.

HONEY CAKES

*1 1/4 lb (575 g) Best semolina * 1/2 Pt. (300 ml) olive oil * Juice and rind 1 orange * 1/2 Teaspoon ground cinnamon * 1 Tablespoon water * 3 oz (75 g) Icing sugar * 2 Liquor glasses cherry brandy * 1/2 Teaspoon baking powder * Pinch ground cloves*
Syrup: *8 oz (225 g) Sugar * 4 fl oz (120 ml) Triple strength rosewater * 8 oz (225 g) Clear honey * 1/2 Pt. (300 ml) Water*

Heat oil and pour this over the semolina. Stir well then add sugar and a little water. When these are well mixed add the orange juice and rind, cherry brandy, baking powder and spices. Knead and shape into round cakes about the size of an egg. Bake on an oiled sheet in a moderate oven for 35 minutes. While cakes are cooking, mix water, honey, rosewater and sugar and boil for 5 minutes, uncovered, in a wide but shallow pan. Remove from heat and put in the freshly baked cakes. Leave for several hours until the syrup has been absorbed by the cakes.

ORANGE MOUSSE

*3 Eggs, separated * 3 oz (75 g) Caster sugar * 2 Tablespoons
cornflour * Grated rind and juice of orange * 1/4 Pt. (150 ml)
Water * 1 Teaspoon lemon juice * 1 oz (25 g) Vegetarian black
margarine, chopped*

Serves 5
Put the yolks, sugar and cornflour into a saucepan, and stir over a low
heat until well mixed. Slowly add the orange rind and juice, the water
and lemon juice, stirring well all the time. Raise the heat and continue
stirring, adding the margarine slowly. Stir until the mixture thickens,
then remove from the heat and leave to cool. Whisk the egg whites
until stiff, then fold them carefully into the cooled orange mixture.
Pour into individual serving dishes and chill for at least one hour before
serving.

6

Middle Eastern Cuisine

The Middle East is a broad fluid term which today means different things to different people. The region embraces many countries, races, and religions. With very few exceptions Arabic is spoken.

People from the Middle East care greatly about their food, the origins of which can be traced back to Bedouin dishes and the peasant meals of the various countries within the region.

Cooking in the Middle East is very traditional and is very much an inherited art. It is not precise and sophisticated as for example Chinese cooking neither is it as experimental as some American cooking is today. Its virtues are loyalty and respect for custom and tradition. This is illustrated by an unswerving attachment to dishes of the past, many of which have been cooked for centuries having remained unchanged from the time they were evolved.

The ingredients must be fresh and of good quality and much time and effort is spent in food preparation. The Middle Eastern diet is extremely healthy and they eat plenty of cereals such as wheat and rice together with pulses and fresh vegetables. Fruit is frequently eaten instead of dessert, although their sweet tooth frequently gives into temptation when offered traditional sweet cakes or pastries soaked in sweet syrup.

Middle Eastern cooking, though somewhat elaborate, is easy and most dishes are prepared in a short time requiring very little hard work. A large number of meals can often be cooked a day in advance and become richer in taste this way.

Chick peas and lentils have been grown for thousands of years in the Middle East and play an important part in the regional diet. Other indigenous plants include figs, dates, melons, pomegranates, cauliflowers etc. As would be expected, spices and herbs feature extensively as in early times that part of the world served as the spice route between the Far East, Africa and Europe. Western society has in recent years developed the capacity to absorb and assimilate these culinary methods.

The dishes very often contain exotic ingredients, many of which will be familiar, but information on some of their uses will be of interest.

Herbs and Spices

Fresh parsley, mint, coriander and dill are frequently used in soups, stews, and salads. Saffron, the world's most expensive spice, is used to flavour and colour rice dishes, stews and some desserts. Sumac, a red spice with a sour lemony flavour is made from the dried berries of the sumac tree and is often used to give colour and sharpness to soup, rice and meat dishes. (Also see Indian cooking, page 45)

CORIANDER

The rounded fruits of this plant are pale in colour, with an aromatic smell, and a taste both sweet and sour, used to season many foods including meats, cheeses, salads, soups, and many puddings and pastries.

CINNAMON

A frequently used Middle Eastern spice and one of the most used for flavouring. It is the bark of the cinnamon tree, and can be purchased in small sticks. It is yellow to brown in colour and has a spicy aroma, and a very fine, sweet, hot taste.

CUMIN

Very distinctive flavour and aroma, taste is between aniseed and fennel, sometimes confused with caraway.

CARDAMOM
Very aromatic, related to the ginger family, comes in large seed pod, white to pale green or brown in colour.

CHERVIL
A herb native to the Middle East, similar to a feathery parsley in appearance, has a hint of parsley and aniseed in its flavour.

MARJORAM
Sweeter than its cousin Oregano, but looses it's flavour quickly if overcooked, so add just a few minutes before serving.

ROSE FLOWER WATER
Very ancient, sweet and heavily scented. Used in salads and meat dishes, as well as sherbets. Buy from a chemist, making sure it is pure.

TURMERIC
The merest pinch will colour a dish bright yellow. A relative of ginger and like that spice a root, although always bought ground. It has a nice light bitter flavour with a hint of hotness.

SAFFRON
The orange stigma from the mauve autumn flowering crocus. Can only be collected by hand and is very expensive. Buy it in strands, a couple will go a long way, too much will give a bitter flavour and too deep a colour. Light primrose yellow and a sweet honey scent is the effect wanted.

Pomegranate Juice or Syrup
This concentrated dark brown liquid is for fruit salads and drinks. It is expensive but well worth trying for its exotic taste.

Nuts
Chopped nuts are used as fillings and toppings for cakes and pastries, whole nuts are frequently fried and are used to decorate rice and savoury dishes.

Phyllo and Kunafeh Pastries

Phyllo (filo) is a thin transparent pastry, when baked it becomes flaky and golden. Kunafeh is a Middle Eastern pastry made from flour and water and looks like white shredded wheat. Both pastries can be bought from Middle Eastern or Greek delicatessens.

Rice

Is served plain or steamed with meat and vegetables, cooked with herbs, decorated with fried nuts and sultanas or used for stuffing vegetables.

Bread

There are many types of bread, leavened and unleavened. It varies in size from thick loaves to thin, flat breads like mankoush, to the well known pitta bread which is flat, soft, and hollow. It is often served with various fillings.

Burghul

Some recipes include burghul, and to make this, whole wheatgrains are partially cooked, then dried and cracked. There are three sizes; medium and large, frequently used for kibbehs and stuffings, and fine burghul which is generally used for kibbehs and salads. Fine burghul should be rinsed before use. The other grains need to be soaked.

Tahini or Tahina

Tahini is a large coloured paste made from ground sesame seeds and it is used to flavour dips and sauces. It is sold in jars and should be stirred before use as the oil separates from the paste.

Mezze Table

A very important aspect of Middle Eastern cooking is the 'mezze table'. This consists of an array of delicious eye catching dips, salads, and small snack dishes, and you will find the flavour of these dishes as mouthwatering as their names suggest.

A mezze table can consist of a small selection of easily prepared time-saving foods, such as nuts, pickles and feta cheese or, for special occasion, a variety of finger dips and other savoury dishes. Many of the favourite mezze courses can also be used as starters for a 3 course meal. A selection of various recipes appear on (pages 116-118) to enable you to experiment and create for your enjoyment your own 'mezze table'.

Desserts

There is a great abundance of fresh fruit in the Middle East and it is frequently served as a dessert. There is an enormous variety to choose from such as, melons, many types of citrus fruits, mangoes, figs, dates, and pomegranates and still many more.

As a contrast, pastries and cakes are extraordinarily sweet, usually made from butter, flour, a variety of nuts such as pistachios, walnuts or almonds, and soaked in a honey rich syrup.

Milk puddings are very popular and are often served with syrup or honey and a scattering of nuts. Halva is the name given to Arabic sweet dishes, particularly those which are like thick pastes. Halva is usually served with coffee or tea and may be eaten with a spoon or cut into pieces. Without a doubt, sweet tooths cannot fail to be satisfied with Middle Eastern cookery.

Drinks

In the Middle East if water is precious, wine is even rarer, especially in the stricter Islamic states, many of which are totally 'dry'. Centuries ago much fine wine was made in the Middle East, and Turkey today still makes some quite acceptable wines. There are, however, many deliciously refreshing drinks made from fruits, rosewater and many other exotic ingredients, such as pomegranates and fruit syrups.

In Middle Eastern countries thick Turkish coffee is drunk throughout the day, sometimes flavoured with crushed cardamoms. In Iraq and Iran however, tea is the most popular drink.

MEZZE AND STARTERS

BAKED STUFFED KIBBEH

Kibbeh: 5 oz (150g) Fine burghul * 11 oz (300g) Finely minced
lamb * 1 Large onion, finely grated * 1 Tsp ground all spice *
Salt, freshly ground black pepper * Oil for glazing
Filling: 1 Medium onion finely chopped * 5 oz (150g) Minced
lamb * 1 Tsp. ground cinnamon * 2 oz (50g) Walnuts, chopped
* 2 oz (50g) Raisins, chopped

Serves 6
Prepare the Kibbeh first. Rinse the burghul well. Pound the meat in a
mortar and paste, or blend in a processor to make a smooth paste.
Work in the burghul, onion, all spice, and seasoning. Chill.
To prepare the filling, fry the onion and meat together until the meat
browns. Add the cinnamon, nuts and raisins. Spread half the kibbeh
over a baking tray. Cover with the filling and top with the remaining
kibbeh smoothing the top with a knife. Cut into diamond shapes and
brush with a little oil. Bake in a fairly hot oven, 200 degrees C, 400
degrees F, Gas 6 for 35-40 minutes until browned. Leave to cool
slightly. Serve hot or cold with salad and yoghurt.

BURGHUL AND HERB SALAD

4 oz (100g) fine burghul * 1 bunch fresh parsley chopped * 2 Tbl
spoons fresh chopped mint * 2 Tomatoes finely chopped * 1
Bunch spring onions finely chopped * 1/2 Onion, grated * 1
Green pepper, de-seeded and finely chopped * 1/2 Lettuce
Dressing: 4 Tablespoons olive oil * Juice of 3 lemons * Salt *
Freshly ground black pepper

Serves 6
Place the burghul in a sieve and rinse with cold water, squeeze out
excess water. Mix together the dressing ingredients. Place all the salad
ingredients, apart from the lettuce, in a bowl, and toss well. Stir in the
dressing. Arrange the lettuce leaves on a serving dish, and pile on the
mixture.

COLD STUFFED VINE LEAVES

*8 oz (225g) Preserved or fresh vine leaves * Juice of 1 lemon*
Stuffing: *5 oz (150g) Short grain rice, rinsed several times * 1
Medium onion, grated * 2 Tablespoons finely chopped parsley *
2 Tomatoes, finely chopped * 1 Teaspoon dried mint * 1/2
Teaspoon All spice * 1/2 Teaspoon ground cinnamon * 1 Clove
garlic, chopped*

Serves 6
Prepare the vine leaves according to instructions on the packet, or
blend fresh leaves in boiling water to soften them. Mix together all the
stuffing ingredients. Place 1 teaspoon of stuffing in the centre of each
leaf. Fold the sides into the middle then roll up the leaf. Line the base
of a large saucepan with damaged leaves to prevent the rest from
sticking. Pack the vine leaves tightly in the pan with the join
underneath. Pour in enough water to cover the leaves, add the lemon
juice, and cover with a small plate. Bring to the boil, then simmer,
covered, for 45 minutes to 1 hour until most of the water has been
absorbed and the rice is tender.

CORIANDER SPICED CRACKED OLIVES

*1 lb (450g) Large green olives * 3 Tablespoons coriander seeds *
3 Garlic cloves, finely chopped * 2 Tablespoons dried oregano *
1/2 Pt. (300ml) Olive oil*

Cut across at the top and bottom of each olive, cutting right through to
the stone. Grind the coriander seeds in a blender, then pack the olives
into jars sprinkling a little coriander seek, some garlic and oregano over
each layer. Leave a good 1 inch (2.5 cm) at the top of the jar and then
fill with olive oil. Cover tightly and leave to marinate for at least 2-3
weeks to let the flavours permeate.

AUBERGINE AND YOGHURT DIP (PITTA BREAD)

*2 Medium aubergines * 2 Cloves garlic, crushed * 1 Tsp salt *
Freshly ground black pepper * 6 Tablespoons tahini * Juice 2
lemons * Olive oil * Paprika * Chopped parsley*

Grill the aubergines until soft, turning occasionally. Strip off the skin
while hot to avoid discolouration of the flesh. Mash the flesh or puree
in a processor. Work in the oil, yoghurt, garlic, salt, pepper, and
lemon juice to make a smooth puree. Serve garnished with a
sprinkling of paprika and parsley.

MIXED VEGETABLE PICKLE

*2 Carrots, sliced * Cauliflower florets, 2 Celery stalks, cut into
chunks * 2 Small red chillies, chopped * Small whole cucumber,
chopped * 1/2 Pt. (300ml) Warm water * 1/2 Pt. (300ml) White
malt vinegar * 2 Tablespoons coarse sea salt * 1 Teaspoon sugar*

Pack the vegetables into large glass jars. Mix together the water,
vinegar, salt and sugar, and stir until the salt and sugar dissolve. Fill the
jars to the top. Cover with a lid, and leave to mature for 2 weeks.

ALMOND DIP

*8 oz (225g) Ground almonds * 3 Garlic cloves, crushed * Pinch
of caster sugar * Juice of 2 lemons * 7 Teaspoons olive oil *
Sea salt * Freshly ground black pepper * 4 Tablespoons chopped
parsley * Paprika*

Serves 6
Mix the almonds with the garlic and a pinch of sugar. Stir in the lemon
juice, then gradually whisk in the oil. Season with salt and black
pepper. Then sprinkle on the parsley. Dribble over a little more oil
then decorate with a pinch or two of paprika.

FISH

FISH KEBABS

2 lb (900g) Sea bass cream, cod, or turbot, filleted * Juice of 4
lemons * Onions, skinned and grated then squeezed to extract
juice * 2 Teaspoons cumin seeds, ground * 2 Garlic cloves, finely
chopped * 1 Teaspoon paprika * Sea salt * Freshly ground
black pepper * 3 Tablespoons olive oil

Serves 6
Cut the fish into chunks about 1 inch (2.5 cm) square, and put in a
large shallow dish. Mix the lemon and onion juices, the cumin, garlic
and paprika with a good pinch of salt and lots of black pepper, then
pour over the fish. Leave for at least 1 hour turning two or three
times. Thread the fish onto skewers, and brush all over with olive oil.
Grill, ideally over charcoal, otherwise under a medium heat for 5-6
minutes, until golden. Serve on a mound of chopped parsley, with
lemon wedges.

FRESH SMOKED FISH WITH CURRIED PEPPER SAUCE

6 Small trout * 2 Tablespoons coriander seeds * 1 Tablespoon
white peppercorns * Sea salt * 6 Cardamom pods, husks * 1
Tablespoon cumin seeds * 1 inch (2.5 cm) fresh root ginger,
peeled & sliced * 1 inch (2.5 cm) piece cinnamon bark * 3 Large
onions, skinned and finely sliced * 6 Tablespoons olive oil
Juice of 2 lemons * 4 Garlic cloves finely chopped * 3 Large
tomatoes, seeded and finely sliced.

Serves 6
Split open trout, clean and wash, but leave the heads and tails on. Put
all the spice, except the ginger and cinnamon into a grinder until fine,
then add the cinnamon and ginger and grind again. Rub the mixture
over the fish - on the flesh side only, and leave to stand for 30 minutes.
Lightly grease a large baking dish, then arrange the fish side by side.
Cover each with a layer of onion, then tomatoes. Mix the oil and
lemon juice with about 6 tablespoons of water and pour over the fish,
then scatter on the garlic. Bake in the oven at 180 degrees C (350 F),
mark 4, for 45 minutes to 1 hour, until the fish is done. Sprinkle with
finely chopped coriander leaves, and serve hot or cold.

GRILLED SWORDFISH STEAKS

*2 1/4 (1 kg) Swordfish, in one piece * Medium onion, skinned and grated, then squeeze to extract the juice * Juice of one large lemon * 1 Tablespoon olive oil * 2 Garlic cloves, crushed * 1 Tablespoon coriander seeds, crushed * Pinch of cayenne pepper * Sea salt*
Dressing: *2 Tablespoons olive oil * 3 Tablespoons lemon juice * 2 Tablespoons finely chopped parsley * Pinch of ground cinnamon*

Serves 6
Skin the fish, then cut into 6 thick steaks, and put these in a large shallow dish. Mix together the onion and lemon juice, olive oil, garlic, coriander seeds, and cayenne pepper, and pour over the fish. Leave to marinate for at least 4-5 hours. Just before cooking, sprinkle the fish with salt, then grill under a high heat for 4 -6 minutes on each side until done right through. Cut the steaks into bite sized pieces, arrange on a large dish, then mix the dressing ingredients together and pour over while the fish is still hot. Serve immediately.

RED MULLET WITH GARLIC

*6 Medium size red mullet, cleaned, cut livers left in * 6 Tablespoons finely chopped parsley * 4 Garlic cloves * Sea salt * Freshly ground black pepper * 3 Tablespoons plain flour * Olive oil*

Serves 6
The livers are a great delicacy, and contribute greatly to the wonderful smoky flavour. Mix the parsley with 2 of the garlic cloves well crushed, then stuff about 1 tablespoon of this into each fish. Crush the remaining garlic with a good pinch or two of salt and a generous grinding of black pepper, then rub all over the skin of the fish. Lightly sprinkle on both sides with flour, then heat a deep fat fryer with a good 2 inches (5 cm) of olive oil until beginning to smoke, cook the fish in the oil, not more than two at a time for 4-5 minutes until thoroughly crispy. Drain well, sprinkle with a little more parsley and serve with lemon wedges.

EGG AND RICE DISHES

CHELO (Rice cooked in butter)

*1 lb (450g) Long grained rice, soaked overnight * Salt * 4 oz (100g) Butter*

Chelo is a very special way of serving rice. The rice is half cooked, then steamed in butter, and a golden crust is formed at the bottom of the pan.
Cleanse the rice, and boil in plenty of salted water for 8 minutes until still chewy. Drain, then rinse in warm water. Melt the butter in a large saucepan, adding 2 tablespoons of water. Spoon the rice carefully into the pan, building it up to form a cone. Make three holes in the rice with a spoon handle to let out the steam. Melt the rest of the butter in a pan, then pour this over the rice. Heat until the steam rises, then cover with a light fitting lid, and cook over a gentle heat for 30 minutes until a crust forms at the bottom. Leave the pan to stand in cold water for 5 minutes to loosen the crust. Serve the white fluffy rice decorated with pieces of crust. Chelo is often served with an egg yolk and sumac.

MEAT EGGAH

*2 Tablespoons olive oil * 1 Large onion, skinned and finely chopped * 2 Garlic cloves, crushed * 14 oz (400g) Minced lamb * Small handful fresh coriander leaves, finely chopped * 1 Teaspoon ground all spice * Salt and freshly ground black pepper * 6 Large eggs * 2 oz (50g) Unsalted butter*

Serves 6
Heat the oil in a frying pan, add the onion and gently saute for 5 minutes until softened. Add the garlic and cook for another 2 minutes, then stir in the meat and fry until browned all over. Tip into a bowl and stir in the coriander, all spice, salt and pepper. Beat the eggs until frothy then blend into the meat. Rinse and dry the frying pan and return to the heat. Melt the butter until just beginning to sizzle, then pour in the egg mixture and cook, covered for about 25 minutes, slowly, until almost set. Put under a very hot grill until golden on top. Serve with a bowl of yoghurt.

AUBERGINE SOUFFLE

*2 Medium aubergines * Juice of 1/2 lemon * Salt and freshly ground pepper * 4 Eggs, separated*

Serves 4

Bake the aubergines in a moderate oven, 180 degrees C, 350 degrees F, Gas 4, until soft, turning once during cooking. While still hot, strip off the skin. Mash the aubergine flesh well, then add the lemon juice and season well. Stir in the egg yolks. In a clean bowl whisk the egg whites until just stiff. Fold in a little of the aubergine mixture, then carefully add the rest. Overheating will flatten the mixture and prevent it from rising. Pour into a greased 8 inch (20 cm) round cake tin, and bake in a fairly hot oven 190 degrees C, 375 degrees F, Gas 5, for 45 minutes until well risen and golden brown. Serve at once with yoghurt and salad or eat cold.

FRESH HERB OMELET

*2 Tablespoons oil * 4 Leeks very finely chopped * 8 oz (225g) Fresh spinach very finely shredded * 2 Tablespoons chopped parsley * 2 Tablespoons finely chopped fresh dill * 2 Cloves garlic, crushed * 1/2 Teaspoon bicarbonate of soda * Salt and freshly ground pepper * 5 Large eggs, lightly beaten*

Serves 4

Heat the oil in an 8 inch omelet pan and gently fry the leeks, spinach, parsley, dill and garlic, stirring and tossing with a wooden spoon until the leeks soften. Set aside to cool a little. Stir the bicarbonate of soda, leek mixture, salt and pepper into the beaten eggs, then return the mixture to the omelet pan, and cook for about 20 minutes until the underside is well browned and crisp and the mixture firm. Turn and cook the other side for about 5 minutes until just beginning to brown. Serve hot or cold.

RICE WITH FRESH HERBS

*1 lb (450g) Long grained rice soaked overnight * 1 Leek, very finely chopped * 2 Tablespoons finely chopped parsley * 2 Tablespoons finely chopped dill * 2 Tablespoons chopped coriander * Salt, freshly ground black pepper * 3 oz (75g) Butter*

Serves 6

Drain the rice and cook in plenty of boiling water for 8 minutes until the rice is still chewy. Drain well, then place in a large bowl. Mix in the leek, parsley, dill, coriander, salt and pepper. Melt half the butter in a large saucepan, adding 2 tablespoons of water.
Carefully spoon in the rice mixture, building it up to form a cone.
Make 3 holes in the rice with a spoon handle to let out the steam. Dot with the remaining butter. Heat until the rice begins to steam, then cover with a tight fitting lid, and cook over a gentle heat for 30 minutes until a crust forms at the bottom. Stand the saucepan in cold water for 5 minutes to loosen the golden crust. Turn the rice out onto a serving dish, crust uppermost. Serve with fish dishes and yoghurt.

MEAT AND POULTRY

CHICKEN WITH POMEGRANATES

4 Chicken breasts, skinned * 4 Tablespoons oil * 2 Medium
onions, sliced into rings * 2 Pomegranates * 2 Tablespoons
pomegranate juice * 2 Tablespoons lemon juice
Garnish: Salt and freshly ground black pepper * 2 oz (50g)
Almonds, cut into strips * Sprigs of parsley

Serves 4
Heat the oil in a pan, and fry the onion rings, and garlic until just
beginning to brown. Remove, then carefully fry the chicken for 7-8
minutes each side. Remove the chicken.
Cut the pomegranates into half and scoop out the red seeds discard
any of the yellow pith. Stir the seeds and juice into the pan with the
lemon juice. Add the onions and enough water to make a thin sauce.
Place the chicken in the sauce, season to taste, cover and simmer for
15 minutes.

FRIED PORK WITH CORIANDER

1 1/2 lb (750g) Boneless pork shoulder * 1 Cup dry red wine * 1
Teaspoon salt * Freshly ground black pepper * 2 Tablespoons
butter * 3 Teaspoons crushed coriander seeds

Serves 4
Cut pork into 3/4 inch (2 cm) cubes, removing any skin. Place in a
glass or ceramic bowl and add the wine, salt and a good grinding of
black pepper. Stir to blend flavours, cover and marinate in refrigerator
for 3-4 hours turning the pork occasionally. Drain the residue pork,
reserving residue. Heat butter in a heavy frying pan, add pork and fry
over high heat, stirring frequently, until browned and just cooked
through. Remove to a plate. Add the pork residue to the pan and
reduce until about 1/4 cup remains. Return pork and sprinkle with
coriander. Toss over heat long enough to heat pork and serve at once,
with salad or vegetables. Serve hot, sprinkled with slivers of almonds,
and garnished with parsley.

CHICKEN STUFFED WITH ALMONDS AND SULTANAS

*3 1/2 lb (1 1/2 kg) Chicken * Salt * 1/4 Pt (150ml) Water * 3 Tablespoons tomato puree*
***Stuffing:** 4 oz (100g) Long grain rice * 2 oz (50g) Flaked almonds * 1 oz (25g) Butter * 3 oz (75g) Sultanas * Juice of half lemon * Freshly grated black pepper * 2 Teaspoons sumac*

Put the skin inside the chicken with salt. To make the stuffing cook the rice for 10 minutes in plenty of boiling water, then drain. Fry the almonds in the butter for 3-4 minutes until golden. Mix together the rice, butter, and almonds, sultanas, lemon juice, salt and pepper and sumac.

Push the stuffing tightly into the chicken, and secure the opening with two skewers. Place the chicken in an ovenproof dish with any remaining stuffing underneath the bird. Mix together the tomato paste and water, and pour this over the chicken.

Cover the dish with foil or a lid and cook in a fairly hot oven, 200 degrees C, 400 degrees F, Gas 6 for 1-1 1/2 hours until the chicken is cooked. Baste occasionally with the tomato liquid, uncover the dish for the final 10 minutes to brown the skin.

ROAST PERSIAN LAMB

*4 lb (1.5 kg) Leg of lamb * 6 Cloves garlic, cut in half lengthways * 4 oz (100g) Butter * 2 Tablespoons tomato puree * 1 Tablespoon fresh chopped mint * 1 Teaspoon turmeric * Salt and freshly ground pepper * 2 Onions, quartered * 3 Carrots, sliced*

Serves 6
Make 12 insertions into the lamb flesh, and into each place half a garlic clove. Put the lamb in a roasting tin. Mix together the butter, tomato puree, mint, turmeric, and salt and pepper. Rub this mixture into the lamb.

Surround the lamb with the onions and carrots and cover with foil. Bake for 30 minutes in a very hot oven, 230 degrees C, 450 degrees F, Gas 5. Baste and turn down the oven to fairly hot, 200 degrees C, 400 degrees F, Gas 6, and cook for another hour. Finally reduce the oven temperature to moderate, 180 degrees C, 350 degrees F, Gas 4, and cook until the lamb is juicy and tender. Leave the meat uncovered for the last 15 minutes for the skin to become crisp.

Serve with salad and rice.

SOUR CHERRY AND MEAT SAUCE

*1 lb (500g) Lean lamb * 1/4 Cup oil * 1 Large onion, finely
chopped * 1/2 Teaspoon turmeric * 1/2 Teaspoon ground
cinnamon * 1/2 Cup water * Salt * Freshly ground black pepper
* 8 oz (250g) Pitted black cherries, sour for preference * 2
Tablespoons lime or lemon juice and enough brown sugar to taste*

Serves 6

Trim meat and cut into 3/4" (2 cm) cubes. Heat half the oil in a heavy
pan and brown meat cubes on each side. Remove meat to a plate.
Reduce heat. Add onion to pan with remaining oil and fry gently until
transparent. Stir in turmeric and cook 2 minutes longer. Return meat
to pan and add cinnamon, water, and salt and pepper to taste. Cover,
and simmer gently for 40 minutes. Add cherries, simmer for 10
minutes to release flavour, then taste sauce. If cherries are sufficiently
sour add one tablespoon of lime or lemon juice and enough brown
sugar to give a pleasant sweet-sour flavour. If sweet cherries are used,
then add more lime or lemon juice and sugar if necessary to balance
the flavour. Cover and simmer for further 20 minutes until meat is
tender. Serve with vegetables, rice, or salad.

STUFFED MEATBALLS

*4 oz (100g) Split yellow lentils * 1 Pint (600ml) Water * 1 lb
(450g) Minced beef * 1 Egg beaten * 1 Teaspoon lemon juice *
1/2 Teaspoon ground cinnamon * 1/4 Teaspoon grated nutmeg *
Salt and freshly ground pepper * 2 Hard boiled eggs * 6 Prunes,
soaked overnight, then stoned*

Cook the lentils in the water for 30-40 minutes until soft. Drain well,
then mash to a puree. Mix together the meat, egg, lemon juice, spices
and salt and pepper to taste in a bowl. Use your hands to work in the
lentil puree. Divide the mixture into two equal portions. Shape into
large balls, putting 1 egg and 3 prunes in the centre of each ball. Place
in a roasting tin half filled with water, and cook for 45-50 minutes in a
moderate oven, 180 degrees F, Gas mark 4 until the meat is cooked.
Serve with chelo rice.
Recipe for chelo rice is on page 121.

DESSERTS

DATE AND PASTRY ROLLS

*4 oz (100g) Unsalted butter * 8 oz (225g) Plain flour * 2 Tablespoons water * Sifted icing sugar*
Filling: *4 oz (100g) Dates, stoned * 1 oz (25g) Butter * 1/2 Teaspoon ground cinnamon * 1 Teaspoon rosewater*

Melt the butter and work it into the flour in a large bowl. Stir in the water, then knead with your hands to form a smooth dough. Cover with cling film, then leave to cool for about 30 minutes.
To make the filling, mince or pound the dates to a smooth paste. Place the dates in a small pan with the butter, cinnamon, and rosewater, and heat gently, stirring until a smooth paste has formed. Spread on a plate to cool. Divide the dough into about 20 pieces, then roll into small balls. Flour the work surface and roll each ball into a 3 inch (7.5 cm) circle.
Place some of the date mixture in a strip down one end, and roll up like a cigar. Place on a greased baking sheet with the join underneath.
Bake in a fairly hot oven, 375 degrees F, 190 degrees C, Gas 5, for 15-20 minutes until a light golden colour. Leave to cool then sprinkle with icing sugar.

STUFFED FRESH DATES

8 oz (225g) Fresh dates
Stuffing: *4 oz (100g) Walnuts * 1/2 Teaspoon mixed spice * A little lemon juice*

Remove the date stones by cutting lengthways with a knife. To make the stuffing, grind the walnuts to a smooth paste, stir in the mixed spice, then add the lemon juice, if necessary, to make the mixture stick together. Roll the stuffing into small sausage shapes and use to stuff into the dates.

HALVA

*1 Teaspoon powdered saffron * 1 Teaspoon sugar * 1/4 Pint
(150 ml) boiling water * 8 oz (225g) Sugar * 1/3 Pint (200 ml) oil
* 1 lb (450g) plain flour * 2 Tablespoons rosewater*
Decoration: *Flaked almonds*

Mix together the saffron and 1 teaspoon of sugar. Boil the ground
saffron, water and sugar in a saucepan until the sugar has dissolved.
Leave to cool. Heat the oil in a saucepan, then stir in the flour, clear
and stir over the heat until the flour starts to change to a golden brown
colour and becomes sandy in texture. This may take 25-35 minutes.
Take care not to burn the mixture. Add the rosewater and 4
tablespoons of the saffron liquid. Cook for a further 10-15 minutes
until the mixture thickens once more. Spread the mixture on a plate,
and decorate with flaked almonds. Cool until firm. Eat with fork or
spoon.

SYRIAN BAKED APPLES

*4 Large cooking apples * 1 oz (25g) ground sweet almonds * 1oz
(25g) Soft brown sugar * 8 oz (225g) Granulated sugar * 2 Purple
figs cut up, small * 1 oz (25g) Coconut, shredded * 1 1/2 oz (40g)
Melted butter * 1/4 Pt. (150 ml) Sweet red wine*

Serves 4
Boil granulated sugar and wine for 10 minutes, uncovered, and stirring
until sugar is dissolved. Remove from the heat and leave aside. Pare
and core the apples and fill the centres with a mixture of figs and
almonds. Roll each apple thoroughly in the melted butter, then in
sugar and coconut mixed. Arrange apples in a baking dish 2 inches (5
cm) high, and surround with the wine syrup. Lower and bake in a
moderate oven for 1 hour. Do not baste during cooking. Serve hot or
cold in own syrup.

PERSIAN PINEAPPLE JELLY

*1/2 Pt. (300 ml) Fresh pineapple juice * 2 Tablespoons cold water
* 1/2 Tablespoon lemon juice * 1 Tablespoon gelatine * 1/4
Teaspoon salt * Fresh pineapple rings * 2 oz (50g) Ratafias,
crushed * 6 oz (175g) Sugar * 1 Small pineapple, crushed * 1/2
Pint (300 ml) Whipped cream * 2 oz (50g) Pistachio nuts*

Serves 4
Heat the pineapple juice. Soften gelatine in cold water and add to the
hot juice. Add sugar and salt and stir until sugar is completely
dissolved. Mix in crushed pineapple and lemon juice, allow to cool,
stirring occasionally until the mixture is partly set. Beat with a rotary
beater for one minute then add the ratajias and the cream. Pour into a
2 pt. (1 litre) mould and chill for 5-6 hours. Unmould and decorate
with rings of fresh pineapple and pistachio nuts.

SWEET POTATO PUDDING

*1 1/2 lb (700g) Sweet potatoes cleaned, peeled and chopped * 2 oz
(50g) Butter * 2 Tablespoons honey * 1 Tablespoon grated *
nutmeg * Pinch of ground ginger * 1/4 Pt. (150 ml) Milk *
2 Eggs, beaten * 2 oz (50g) Chopped dates*

Serves 6
Boil the sweet potatoes in water for 20 minutes until soft. Drain, then
mash them with butter. Beat in the honey, nutmeg and ginger. Mix
together the milk and eggs, and stir into the mixture. Pour into a
greased ovenproof dish, and sprinkle with chopped dates. Bake in a
moderate oven, 180 degrees C, 350 degrees F, Gas 4 for about 45
minutes until the pudding is firm. Serve hot with cream.

DRINKS

BUTTERMILK DRINK

*1 Pt. (600 ml) Buttermilk * Pinch of salt * 1 Pt. (600 ml) Soda water * Freshly ground allspice*

Makes 2 Pts (1.1 Ltr)
Whisk the buttermilk with a good pinch of salt, then chill for 1-2 hours. Add chilled soda water to taste, a few ice cubes, and a generous sprinkling of allspice.

ARAB COFFEE

*4 Tablespoons (60 ml) Turkish or espresso coffee * 1 Cardamom pod, husk removed and seeds ground * 2 Cloves ground*

Makes 5 small cups
Bring 1/2 Pt. (300 ml) of water just to boiling point in a small pan. Take off the heat, sprinkle on the coffee and spices, lightly stir once, then return to the stove and simmer gently until the coffee begins to froth. Lift up high above the heat again until it foams once more. Stir. Return to the heat for one more frothing, then take off and let it stand for one minute to let some of the grounds sink. Pour into small cups, giving each person some of the froth. Do not stir the coffee once it is in the cups. This is a delicately spiced but very strong brew.

MINTED TEA

*2 Tablespoons (30 ml) Earl Grey * 4 oz (100g) Caster sugar * Small bunch fresh mint*

Rinse the teapot with boiling water (unless it is silver), then add the tea and pour in about 1 Pt. (600 ml) of boiling water. Infuse for about 9 minutes, then pour into a jug and cool. Chill for one hour, then serve in tall glasses with a sprig of fresh mint in each.

POMEGRANATE SHERBET

*2-3 Large pomegranates * 6 oz (175g) Caster sugar * 1 Teaspoon roseflower water*

Makes 2 Pts. (1.1 Ltr)
Squeeze the pomegranates all over, pressing hard with the fingertips. You should feel the pips being crushed inside, and the fruit will become quite pulpy and soft to the touch. Holding the pomegranate inside a deep bowl, carefully make a slit in the skin with a very sharp knife. Squeeze gently to extract all the juice. Dissolve the sugar in one pint (600 ml) of water. Taste to see if you need more sugar. Pour into a jug and chill well. Add some ice cubes, sprinkle on the rose flower water.

YOGHURT DRINK

*1 Pt. (600ml) Natural yoghurt * Sea salt * 4 Tablespoons fresh mint*

Makes 2 Pts. (1.1 Ltr)
Whisk the yoghurt in a large jug, then pour in 1 pint (600 ml) water, constantly heating. Add a pinch of salt, then whisk in the mint - you can make the whole drink in a blender if you wish, for a smooth, frothy effect. Chill for at least one hour, then add some ice cubes to the jug and serve in long tall glasses.

7
Spanish Cuisine

Occupying most of the Iberian peninsula from the Pyrenees to the Straits of Gibraltar, Spain is a country with a rich history, remarkable scenery and a cuisine as varied as its landscape.

The invasion of Spain by the Moors in the 15th century left an indelible mark on Spanish cooking. It is not generally known that many of the basic ingredients of modern cooking, such as almonds, lemons, many spices, tomatoes, potatoes, pepper and chocolate were all introduced to Europe by the Moors.

Spanish cooking developed by utilising the abundance of the ingredients that became available. Cooking generally owes a debt to Spain not only for the imaginative use of these, but also for the creation of many of the best loved Mediterranean dishes we all enjoy today. The Spaniards created puff pastry and nougat. Genuine and legitimate Spanish dishes are excellent and are as wholesome as any in the world.

Spanish food, whether it graces the poor man's kitchen or the rich man's dining table is by nature 'del Pueblo' (of the people). It is never classical cooking in the sense of 'Grande Cuisine'.

Spanish recipes can be rather complex at times, but the ingredients are never disguised and never spiced to alter basically simple tastes. The strength of Spanish cooking is in its naturalness'. Its subtlety of flavours is derived from the combination of ingredients. This makes dishes highly distinctive and you will not be likely to mistake them for anything else. The cooking is usually plain and attractively appetising in the simplest possible way. Dishes are rarely decorated, paella being a notable exception. They are fresh and are concerned more with quality ingredients well combined than with additives.

BASIC DISHES

Paella

Paella is to Spain as pasta is to Italian cooking. It is undoubtedly the most famous national dish and is a masterpiece of flavours which is spectacularly presented steaming in a large iron pan.

The name paella originates from the double handed pan in which it is cooked. It is prepared with different ingredients in different regions of Spain. Vegetables, meat, chicken and sausage are the main ingredients in the interior, whilst Valencia and Barcelona specialise in combining sea foods with chicken and vegetables in a rice base.

If you are visiting Spain, this is an experience not to be missed.

Recipes for paella from two different regions are on pages 145 and 149.

Soups

Soups are a very popular first course throughout Spain. Fish, as would be expected, features prominently and there is also a vast range of country soups where vegetables and meat are the main ingredients.

The 'Sopa de Pescado' (fish soup), although not as elaborate as the French Boulibaisse, is very highly regarded. The flavours of the various fish combined with a mixture of herbs and seasonings create quite a unique and delightful piquancy. Two recipes of fish soups from different regions are included in the soup dishes together with a selection of other traditional and well known ones.

Spain is famous for its Gazpacho soup which is served chilled or hot. It is easily prepared, and is an ideal accompaniment to a summer time meal.

The soups recipes on page 139 include two regional as well as traditional and universally known recipes.

Fish

Because Spain has extensive coastlines on both the Mediterranean and the Atlantic, fish and shellfish have always been popular and used extensively in Spanish cooking.

One of the best known fish dishes is Zarzuela which takes its name from a Spanish word meaning a variety show. It is truly magnificent and offers a variety of shellfish and firm white fish, cooked in a rich sauce containing onions, garlic and tomatoes (recipe page 146). Some of the most popular fish dishes from various regions of Spain have been included to give the opportunity of sampling and enjoying the different methods of food preparations. These include from Andalusia, 'Fillets of Turbot Andalusian Style' (page 144); from Catalonia, 'Catalan Hake' (page 143); and from Bilbao, 'Bilbao Squid' (page 143).

Meat and Poultry

The Spanish in general have healthy appetites and derive a great deal of pleasure from hearty meat and poultry dishes. Beef and pork are in the main the most popular meats and a number of dishes have been created which illustrate the true flavour and pleasure of traditional Spanish cooking. There is for instance 'Fillets of Pork Baturra' (recipe page 147) which combines the flavours of red wine, smoked ham, olives and other ingredients to produce a most delightfully tasty dish. Chicken and duck are extremely popular and it is most unlikely that you will see a Spanish menu where either one or the other or both are not offered. The creative ability of Spanish cooks with poultry is illustrated in 'Chicken with Raisins and Pine Nuts' (recipe page 147) and 'Duck with Caper Sauce' (recipe page 148), which includes among its ingredients almonds and olives.

Eggs

Egg dishes are very popular in Spanish cuisine and they are prepared and served in a number of unusual and imaginative ways. The 'Spanish omelette' (recipe page 141) for instance which is enjoyed throughout Spain is entirely different from the traditional French one. The ingredients are usually potato, onion and garlic or a mixture of vegetables. It is served round and flat as opposed to the usual 'roll over' presentation. 'Eggs in Breadcrumbs' (recipe page 142) includes a dash of sherry and 'Eggs Flamenco' (recipe page 141) is a tasty and exciting concoction including amongst other ingredients, peppers, garlic, and asparagus tips. Do try the recipes in the Egg section as you will discover a completely unique and enjoyable way to serve and enjoy eggs.

Desserts

Desserts are very much an integral part of a Spanish meal. Spaniards are great lovers of ice-cream. Most dishes cater for the Spanish love of sweet things. One of the most well known of desserts is 'Baked Custard with Brittle Caramel' (recipe page 150). This is a delightfully light and pleasant dish, the delicate taste of the custard combined with the crunch of the caramel is a pleasure to be savoured. Also included is 'Pumpkin Dessert' (recipe page 151) which again illustrates the Spanish ability to create attractive dishes from unusual ingredients. You will frequently see on Spanish menus, 'Dried Fruit and Nuts' which is another popular way of completing a Spanish meal.

Cheese

The cheeses of Spain like the cuisine are of great variety. In the north and north west, where the countryside is green and lush, most cheeses are made from cows' milk because of the ideal grazing conditions.

In the other parts of Spain where it is hot and arid and the terrain is not suitable for cattle, sheep and goats are reared, their milk being used for cheese making.

The notion that Spanish cheese is 'bland' is quite unfounded, as a number of excellent cheese are produced.

MACHENGO

Has for centuries been Spain's most popular cheese. It is made from herb scented sheeps' milk. Creamy white and firm.

RONCAL
Another hard cheese. Cows' milk. Salted and smoked. Tangy taste. Keeps well.

SIMON
Semi hard smoked farmhouse cheese. Tastes fine and creamy, slightly sourish. Cows' milk.

QUESO BELLUSCO
Sheeps' milk. Hard cheese from Asturias. Rough crust, pleasant sharp flavour.

ARAGON
Mixture of sheep and goats' milk. Semi-hard. Pleasant smooth creamy taste.

VILLALON
Pressed by hand and steeped in brine for a few hours, then packed in chip wood boxes. Fresh sharp taste. Sheeps' milk.

BURGOS
Named after the town. White cheese with no rind. Fresh light taste and characteristic aroma of sheeps' milk cheese.

UOLLA
Semi hard, mild taste. Ripened outside, protected from the sun and dried by the wind.

Vinos (Wine)
Spain has more land under vine than any other country, but does not produce the most wine. It does, in fact, hold third place behind Italy and France.

There have been dramatic changes in the Spanish wine industry over the past few years, and the range and quality is now comparable with the best that any other country can produce.

The most highly regarded wines are those from the areas of Rioja, Valdepenas, Perialada and Pemedes, but many excellent

wines are grown in other areas. The Rosados (Roses) make a
particularly pleasant accompaniment to a light summer time meal.
A visit to your local off-license to discuss with the patron the
various wines he has available is recommended, as doubtless he will
be able to suggest an appropriate wine that will more than do
justice to whatever meal you had in mind.

Champagne

The term 'champagne' referring to sparkling wines is now
illegal, one of the reasons being that true champagne comes from
the tiny 'pinot noir' or 'pinot blanc' grapes grown in the
champagne district of France, and no 'pinot' grapes are grown in
Spain.

That said, the sparkling wines of Spain make an excellent
accompaniment to a complete meal and it is best to ignore any
ill-founded remarks you may have heard about them. It is a drink
very much to be savoured and enjoyed.

As a point of interest, there is a huge export trade of sparkling
wines to the U.S.A. and the quality of these are impressive, even to
the champagne makers of France.

SOUPS

ALMOND SOUP

*14 oz (400g) Roasted almonds * 2 oz (50 g) Castor sugar * 1 Stick cinnamon * Peel of 1 lemon in a single piece * 1 oz (25g) Bread, cut up small*

Grind the almonds in mincer. Add to a saucepan containing 1 3/4 Pts (1 ltr) of water, together with the cinnamon and lemon peel. Bring the water to the boil and simmer for 5 minutes, then add the bread and cook for another 10 minutes until the bread has disintegrated and the liquid is smooth. Remove the lemon peel and serve very hot.

FISH SOUP (CATALONIA)

*1 lb (1/2k) Firm white fish * Salt * Olive oil * 2 Onions, chopped * 7 oz (200g) Tomatoes, blanched peeled and chopped * 1 Clove garlic, crushed * 1 Teaspoon parsley chopped * 1 Small packet saffron * 2 oz (50g) Almonds, shelled * 2 oz (50g) French bread, thinly sliced*

First, cover the fish with cold salted water and simmer for about 10 minutes. Then drain, reserving the stock. Put the fish on a plate, remove the skin and bones, then cut up the fish and reserve. Heat a little olive oil in another saucepan, fry the onions until golden, drain off excess oil, then stir in the chopped tomatoes, parsley and garlic. Meanwhile pound the saffron and almonds in a mortar so as to make a paste. Add this and the fish stock to the contents of the saucepan, together with a little more water and salt if necessary, and simmer for 1/2 hour. Strain the liquid through a sieve, return it to the pan, add the pieces of fish, check the seasoning and once the saucepan is on the boil again drop in the sliced bread. Remove from heat without delay, cover with a lid and leave for 5 minutes before serving.

ROYAL SOUP

*4 oz (100g) Smoked ham * 1 Cooked breast of chicken * 3 Hard boiled eggs * 1 Wine glass dry sherry * 3 Pints (1.75 Lt) Stock * Salt and pepper*

Serves 4
Chop up the chicken and ham very fine, also the hard boiled egg, put into a warmed soup tureen, pour the hot stock and sherry over and serve with croutons.

CHILLED GAZPACHO

*2 lb (1 kg) Tomatoes * 2 Onions * 1 Lemon * 1 Clove garlic *
2 Red peppers * 2 Tablespoons oil * 2 Tablespoons vinegar *
Salt and pepper*

Serves 4
Wash the tomatoes, peel the onions, wash the lemon and cut in half to
extract the pips. Clean the peppers of all inner seeds. Put all this in
the liquidiser with the garlic, oil and vinegar. Season to taste with salt
and pepper and a pinch of sugar. Put in refrigerator to cool. Serve
with finely diced cucumber, tiny pieces of white bread or toast and
finely chopped onion.

HOT GAZPACHO

*1 lb (1/2 kg) Tomatoes * 4 Cloves garlic * 1 Green pepper, cut
small * 4 Tablespoons refined olive oil * 1 Teaspoon salt * 1
1/4 Pts (3/4 Ltr) Water from cooking the tomatoes * 2 oz (50g)
Brown breadcrumbs * 1/2 Teaspoon sweet paprika powder*

Boil the tomatoes in the water for 10 minutes. Pour off and reserve
the water, cover the tomatoes with cold water, remove the skins and
put tomatoes on a plate. Grind the garlic and pepper in a large bowl,
then add the blanched tomatoes, olive oil and salt. Make a puree of the
mixture by rubbing it through a sieve or putting it in a blender and
adding the breadcrumbs, together with the sweet paprika and half of
the reserved water. Now transfer to a soup dish, sift until thoroughly
mixed and pour in the rest of the water at the boil. Serve very hot.

GALLEGO SOUP

*8 oz (225g) White beans * Knuckle bone of brace Veal bone *
8oz (225g) Boiling beef * 1 White cabbage * 4 Potatoes * Salt
and pepper*

Serves 6
Soak beans overnight in cold water. Put 7 pints (4 Lt) water to boil in a
saucepan, add beans, bacon and veal bones and minced beef. Bring to
the boil and take off film, then simmer for 2-3 hours. Add shredded
cabbage and diced potatoes, season to taste, remove bones and serve.

EGGS

SPANISH POTATO OMELETTE

*6 Eggs * 1 Onion * Salt and pepper * 1 lb (450g) Potatoes *
Oil for frying*

Serves 3
Chop up the onion and fry until golden. Peel and dice the potatoes.
Slowly fry these until tender, but not crisp. Beat the eggs well with a
few drops of water. Take care not to leave too much oil in the pan.
Place the potatoes and onions in and pour the eggs over. When done
on one side, carefully turn over by slipping onto a saucepan lid and
putting a little more oil into the pan, return to the pan. Serve
immediately. All Spanish omelettes are served flat, not rolled over.

EGGS FLAMENCA STYLE

*6 Eggs (or 2 each if required) * 2 lb (1 kg) Tomatoes * 8 oz (225g)
Small peas (petit pois) * 8 oz (225g) Green beans * 8 oz (225g)
Asparagus tips * Olive oil * 6 Slices ham * Salt and pepper *
4 oz (100g) Chopped ham * 4 oz (100g) Garlic sausage * 1 Onion
* 2 Garlic cloves * 1 Teaspoon chopped parsley * 1/2 Pt. (300
ml) Stock * 3 Sweet peppers (canned) * Dash of sugar*

Serves 6
Heat the oil in a saucepan and slightly fry the onion and garlic, but do
not allow to brown, add the chopped ham, the peppers and the
tomatoes cut into slices, season with salt and pepper and a dash of
sugar. Add the stock, cut into small pieces and add the green beans
and the peas. Cook slowly, until tender. Place the cooked vegetables
in a baking dish, break the eggs over them, spacing them well, garnish
with the garlic sausage and strips of ham and tinned red peppers.
Place at the bottom of a hot oven so that the whites set quickly, leaving
the yolks liquid. Serve immediately with strips of fried bread. Eggs
flamenca are suitable for little individual dishes.

EGGS IN BREADCRUMBS

*7 Eggs * Breadcrumbs * Oil for frying * Tomato sauce*

Serves 6
Poach 6 eggs and carefully cut the white to make them even and round. Dip into breadcrumbs. Beat up 1 egg and dip the eggs into this and then again into the breadcrumbs. Salt and fry until golden. Serve with a thick tomato sauce, prepared with tomato puree and a dash of sherry.

EGGS RANCHERO

*4 oz (100g) Minced meat * 1 Onion * 4 Eggs * Olive oil * 1 Small can tomato puree * 10 oz (275g) Plain boiled rice*

Serves 4
Fry the chopped onions together with the mincemeat. When brown add the tomato puree, slightly diluted with water. Simmer gently. Fry the eggs in the ordinary way. Line 4 individual dishes with rice, place the fried egg in the centre, and over it the meat and tomato sauce. Serve immediately.

SPANISH POTATO SOUFFLE

*4 Large potatoes * 8 oz (225g) Butter * 1/4 Pt. (150 ml) Cream * 4 oz (100g) Lean smoked ham * 4 Egg yolks * 6 Egg whites * Salt and pepper * 2 Tablespoons melted butter*

Serves 8
Boil the potatoes in their skins. Peel and mash well while hot in a deep dish, season, add the butter over a low heat, beating well. Add the cream little by little and season. Remove from the heat and add the finely chopped ham and the yolks. Beat well. Exactly 20 minutes before required, add the whites of egg beaten to stiff snow, pour into buttered dish and bake in a hot oven for about 20 minutes. Serve immediately.

FISH

BILBAO SQUID

*24 Small squid * 2 Onions * 2 Tomatoes * Salt and pepper *
1 Tablespoon olive oil * 1 Clove garlic * 2 oz (50g) Breadcrumbs
* 1 Teaspoon chopped parsley*

Serves 4
Cut the squid in several pieces, separate the ink bags carefully and
place the liquid in a cup. Heat the oil in a saucepan and slightly fry the
chopped onion, chopped garlic, tomatoes (previously peeled) and
chopped parsley. Put the squids in this, adding sufficient water to
cover. Simmer until tender. In the meanwhile stir the ink with the
breadcrumbs, salt and pepper, adding a little of the ink, stir well while
slowly bringing to the boil. Serve with slices of fried bread and boiled
rice.

CATALAN HAKE

*4 Thick hake fillets * 4 Pieces fried bread * Anchovy butter *
8 Fl oz (250ml) Tomato sauce * 2 Teaspoons chopped parsley *
Oil for frying*

Serves 4
Clean and dry the fillets. Fry four pieces of bread in oil the same size
as the fillets. Grill the fillets and place each one on a piece of fried
bread which you have spread with anchovy butter. Serve on individual
plates with tomato sauce. Sprinkle with parsley.

CREAM SOLE SPANISH STYLE

*4 Fillets dover sole * Grated Cheese * 1/2 Pt (300 ml) Milk *
2 Eggs * 2 Tablespoons flour * Salt and pepper * Lemon juice*

Serves 4
Place the fillets in boiling water with salt and lemon juice. Take care to
keep the fillets whole. Place on heated serving dish, sprinkle with
grated cheese. In the meantime, make a custard cream. Beat up the
white of the eggs until stiff, then beat the yolks into the milk and
carefully add the flour, simmer for a moment to heat, and fold in the
whites. Season to taste, and pour over the boiled fillets. Serve
immediately

FILLETS OF TURBOT ANDALUSIAN STYLE

*6 Fillets of turbot * 1 Piece of fish (for stock) * 2 Onions * 8 oz (225g) Tomatoes * 4 oz (100g) Mushrooms * 2 Sweet peppers * 4 oz (100g) Butter * 2 Tablespoons breadcrumbs * 1 Garlic clove * Chopped parsley * Salt and pepper * 1 Wine glass white wine*

Serves 6

Flatten the fillets with a wooden spoon, place in a baking dish, spread with butter and keep in a cool place until ready to use. Boil piece of fish with one onion and salt in sufficient water to cover. while boiling, add wine. To make good stock simmer for about 20 minutes. In the meantime chop the onion and garlic clove, clean and chop the sweet peppers, peel and cut the mushrooms, wash and cut the tomatoes into small pieces. Fry the onion until golden, then add the peppers and mushrooms. When these are tender add the tomatoes. Pour the stock, of which there should be about two tumblers full, over the turbot and over this the fried vegetables. Bake in a fairly hot oven for 25 minutes. The fish will be tender and the stock absorbed, but the dish will not be dry. To enhance the taste, a little lemon juice should be added before serving.

PRAWNS WITH GARLIC

*8 oz (225g) Large peeled prawns * 3 Garlic cloves, peeled * 2 Tablespoons olive oil * Paprika * 2 Tablespoons dry sherry * 2 Teaspoons lemon juice * Salt and pepper*

Serves 4

Finely chop 1 garlic clove and, using a pestle and mortar or small bowl, and the back of a spoon, mash the garlic to a paste. Gradually whisk in 2 teaspoons of oil, beating well until the mixture reaches the consistency of mayonnaise. Heat the remaining oil in a medium sized frying pan over a high heat. Add the remaining 2 garlic cloves and a sprinkling of paprika and saute until the garlic turns golden brown, about 1 minute.

(Take care not to burn the garlic). Remove and discard the garlic. Add the prawns to the hot oil and saute 1-2 minutes on each side. Add the sherry, lemon juice, salt and pepper and cook for 1 minute. Add the garlic and oil mixture and stir well to combine. Serve at once.

PAELLA

*1 Tablespoon olive oil * 1 Garlic clove, finely chopped *
1/2 Red and 1/2 green pepper, seeded and cut into thin strips *
1 Onion, finely chopped * 14 oz (420g) Skinned and boned
chicken breasts, cut into 1/2 (cm) strips * 2 Tomatoes, peeled and
chopped * 4 oz (100g) Long grain rice * Good pinch powdered
saffron * Approximately 12 Fl oz (360 ml) boiling water *
1/4 Teaspoon salt * 4 oz (100g) Peeled prawns * 8 Unpeeled
prawns * 6 oz (180g) Frozen peas * 8 Large mussels, steamed *
Chopped parsley to garnish*

Serves 4
Heat the oil in a saucepan, deep frying pan or paella pan. Add the
garlic, peppers and onion and cook 2-3 minutes. Add the chicken and
saute over a medium heat until the chicken loses its pink colour, stirring
all the time. Stir in the tomatoes, and rice and cook for a further 2
minutes. Add the peeled prawns and peas and cook for a further five
minutes or until the rice is cooked through. Add the mussels and heat
through. Sprinkle with the chopped parsley, garnish with the unpeeled
prawns.

SEAFOOD STEW (Zarzuela)

Sofrito Sauce: *3 Onions grated* * *2 Tablespoons olive oil* *
2 Large ripe tomatoes, peeled de-seeded and finely chopped *
Salt
Picada Sauce: *3 Thin slices white bread, crusts removed, fried in
oil* * *6 Blanched almonds, toasted* * *3 Garlic cloves* * *1 Large
monkfish tail, cut into 6 pieces* * *Flour* * *Olive oil for frying* *
10 oz (300g) Squid, cleaned and cut into rings * *3 Small lobsters,
(about 14 oz)* * *6 Prawns* * *6 King Prawns* * *24 Mussels cleaned
thoroughly* * *2 Garlic cloves finely chopped* * *Large bunch of
parsley, finely chopped* * *7 Fl oz (200 ml) Brandy* * *12 Large
clams, cleaned*

Serves 6
Start by making the 2 sauces. To make the sofrito, gently fry the
onions in the oil until soft and just beginning to colour. Add the
tomatoes and salt and cook for 10 mins. stirring constantly. Add 4 fl
oz (125 ml) of water, stir and continue to cook until the sauce is thick
but still quite liquid. Keep aside. To make the picada. Pound the
bread to a paste with the almonds and garlic or blend them in a food
processor. Keep aside. Coat the fish pieces with flour & fry in shallow
oil in a large frying pan until they are brown. Transfer to a large
shallow preferably earthenware casserole. Very quickly, fry the squid.
Fry the lobsters and prawns until they turn pink. (Cooked lobsters and
prawns do not need frying). Fry the mussels and clams until they open.
Transfer the seafood as they are cooked to the casserole. Sprinkle in
the chopped garlic and the parsley. Pour the brandy into the casserole
and flame. When the flames die down pour in sofrito sauce and add 4
Fl oz (125 ml) water, then put the casserole over a gentle heat for 4
minutes. Stir in the picada, check the reasoning and cook, for another
five minutes.

MEAT AND POULTRY

CHICKEN WITH RAISINS AND PINE NUTS

*1 1/2 lb (750g) Boned chicken * 2 Tablespoons raisins * 6 Fl oz (175 ml) Dry sherry * 2 Tablespoons butter * 1 1/2 Tablespoons olive oil * Salt and pepper * 2 Tablespoons pine nuts*

Serves 4
Put the raisins to soak in the sherry. Heat the butter and 1 tablespoon of oil in a frying pan and, when the mixture begins to sizzle, put in the chicken. Lower the heat and cook gently for a few minutes until lightly browned, turning the pieces over at least once. Add salt and pepper, pour in the sherry with the raisins and simmer very gently over a low heat, covered for about 20 minutes or until the chicken is done. Make sure that the bottom does not stick and add a little water if necessary. Fry the nuts in the rest of the oil until lightly coloured, drain them on kitchen paper, then stir them in with the chicken. Serve hot.

CREAMED TOURNEDOS

*6 Beef tornedos * 4 Tablespoons oil * 1 Onion * 1 Tablespoon flour * Salt and pepper * 1/4 Pt (150 ml) Milk * 1 Egg yolk * 1 Teaspoon chopped parsley * Juice of a lemon * Butter*

Serves 6
Fry the tornedos in oil, season and keep warm while preparing the sauce. Fry the finely chopped onion in butter, add the flour and the milk, stir until thick and add the beaten yolk, the parsley and the lemon juice, season and pour over the tornedos. Serve with boiled potatoes.

FILLETS OF PORK BATURRA

*2 Fillets of pork * Flour * 1 Wine glass red wine * Oil for frying * 1 Onion * 4 oz (100g) Smoked ham * 24 Olives * 1 Tablespoon tomato puree * 2 Hard boiled eggs*

Serves 4
Flour the fillets and fry in hot oil until golden, and well done all through. Drain well and keep hot. In the same oil, fry the chopped onion and ham. Mix the tomato puree with the wine and a little flour to thicken the sauce, add and stir while simmering. Add the meat again and, at the last moment, the chopped olives. These should not boil as they would get hard. Garnish with finely sliced hard boiled egg.

MADRID PORK CHOPS

*4 Pork chops * 4 Tablespoons olive oil * Parsley * 2 Garlic cloves * 1 Bay leaf * Marjoram * 1 Red pepper * Salt and pepper*

Serves 4

Chop the garlic and parsley, add the oil, bay leaf, marjoram, sliced red pepper and salt and pepper. Put the chops in this, and cover the dish. Turn the chops from time to time so that the herbs can penetrate both sides. Bake in a medium to hot oven, basting so that the chops do not get dry. Serve with fried potatoes.

ROAST ROUND OF VEAL

*2 lb (1 kg) Best veal * 4 oz (100g) Lard * 2 Onions * 2 Carrots * Bay leaf * 2 Rashers bacon * 1 Small can tomato puree * 4 Tomatoes * 1 Glass dry white wine * Parsley * Salt and pepper*

Serves 4

Wrap the rashers around the veal, place in a roasting tin, add the sliced onions, carrots and the lard,, and roast in a moderately hot oven. When half done, add the wine, bay leaf, and sliced tomatoes. Cover the roasting tin and return to a moderate oven, cook for 2 hours. When done, put the sauce through a sieve. Season and re-heat. Carve and place on a serving dish, garnish with fried potatoes and parsley and serve sauce separately.

DUCK WITH CAPER SAUCE

*1 Duck * 2 Onions * 4 oz (100g) Butter * 3 oz (75g) Stoned olives * 3 oz (75g) Stoned raisins * 1 oz (25g) Capers * 1oz (25g) Blanched almonds * 4 Tomatoes * Salt*

Serves 6

Wash duck well and boil with an onion and salt. Carve into pieces and take off the bone., Melt the butter in a casserole, chop an onion and fry with peeled tomatoes. When done, add the pieces of duck and simmer. Add the almonds, capers, olives and raisins. Add sufficient hot stock from the duck to just cover. Simmer until much of the stock has evaporated and the remaining sauce is thick. Serve hot.

SOUSED HARE

*Hare * Olive oil * 6 Carrots * 2 Onions * 1 Wine glass dry
white wine * 1 Lemon * 3 Chopped garlic cloves *
1/2 Teaspoon peppercorns * 4 Fl oz (120 ml) Vinegar *
2 Tomatoes * Salt * 1 Bouquet herbs*

Serves 6
Cut the hare into large pieces, salt, and slightly brown in oil, place in a
large casserole with the sliced carrots, onions, garlic, herbs,
peppercorns, vinegar, wine, 1/4 Pt. (150 ml) oil. Cover the casserole
and cook until the hare is tender. By then, the sauce will be thick, and
greatly reduced. Prepared in this way, the hare is just as delicious cold
as it is hot. Serve with slices of lemon.

VALENCIAN PAELLA

*1/2 Chicken, about 1 1/2 lb (750g) * 1 1/2 lb lean pork or ham *
5 Tablespoons olive oil * 2 Ripe tomatoes, peeled and chopped *
4 oz (125 g) White Spanish beans or butter beans, soaked over
night * 8 oz (250g) Green beans, topped & tailed, and strings
removed, cut into pieces * 2 Teaspoons paprika * 2 Sprigs
rosemary * 1/2 Teaspoon saffron * Salt * 1 1/2 lb (750g) Short
grain rice*

Serves 6
Cut the chicken and meat into small pieces, fry in the oil in a large
frying pan until lightly browned. Add the tomatoes drained, butter
beans and green beans. Sprinkle with paprika, rosemary, saffron and
salt. Cover with water and simmer for 45-60 minutes until the meat is
very tender. Add the rice, stir well and cover with enough water to
make up about 3 pts. (1.75 ltr) of liquid and cook first on a high heat
for about 10 minutes, then reduce the heat and cook until the rice is
tender but still relatively firm and separate, add water if it becomes dry
too quickly or turn the heat up to dry it and if it is still wet at the end.
Cover it with a lid and let it rest for 5 minutes before serving.

DESSERTS

BAKED CUSTARD WITH BRITTLE CARAMEL

*6 Egg yolks * 1 oz (25g) Cornflour * 11 oz (320g) Icing sugar *
1 Fl oz (1/2 ltr) Milk * 1 Cinnamon stick * Peel of 1 lemon*

Beat the egg yolks in a bowl with the cornflour and 6 oz (170g) of the
icing sugar. Simmer the milk with the cinnamon stick and lemon peel,
then add the egg mixture and cook slowly, stirring continuously to
avoid lumps, until the custard thickens. Now remove the cinnamon
and lemon peel, pour the custard into a serving dish and leave to cool.
Finally, sprinkle the surface with the rest of the icing sugar and press
lightly on it with a palette knife, heated on a gas flame, so as to form a
brittle layer of caramel on the top.

SPANISH ORANGE CREAM

*2 oz (50g) Sugar * 5 Eggs * 1/2 Pt (300 ml) Milk * 1/2 Pt (300
ml) Orange juice, with juice of 1/2 lemon*

Serves 6
Put the sugar in a double saucepan and beat up the yolks of 4 eggs
together with the orange juice and add to the sugar. Beat 1 whole egg
up with the milk and add. Beat all the time over a moderate heat until
it has turned into a thick, frothy cream.

PUMPKIN DESSERT

*Piece of pumpkin approx 3 lb (1.5k) * Grated rind of 1 Lemon *
1 Teaspoon cinnamon * 8 oz (250g) Sugar to taste * 7 oz (200g)
Ground almonds*
Decoration: *2 oz (50g) Blanched almonds * 2 Tablespoons pine
nuts * Icing sugar * Cinnamon*

Serves 10
Preheat the oven to 400 degrees F, 200 degrees C, Gas mark 6. Cut
the pumpkin into large pieces and scrape out the seeds and loose
fibres. Place the pieces in a baking dish, cover with foil and bake for
20 minutes or until the pumpkin feels tender when you pierce it with
the point of a knife. Cut away the skin and mash the flesh, then put it
in a colander and squeeze out as much of the juice as you can. Lower
the oven temperature to 300 degrees F, 150 degrees C, Gas 2. Beat
the eggs with the lemon rind, cinnamon, and sugar and mix in the
ground almonds. Add the mashed pumpkin and mix very well. Oil a
large ovenproof dish and pour in the mixture. Bake for 1 hour or until
it feels firm, and the top is gently coloured. Stick the almonds, pointing
upwards, into the dessert. Scatter pine nuts over the top and dust with
icing sugar and cinnamon. Serve cold.

INDEX

153

Duck with Pineapple AC, 22

E

Eel Ferrara Style IT, 80
Eggs in Breadcrumbs SP, 142
Eggs Flamenca SP, 141
Eggs Stuffed with Mushrooms JE, 97
Eggs Ranchero SP, 142
Escalopes with Black Olives GR, 36
Exotic Fried Rice IN, 49

F

Feta GR, 42
Fillets of Pork Buturra SP, 147
Fillets of Turbot Andalusian Style
SP, 144
Fish Fillets on Skewers GR, 34
Fish Roe Cakes GR, 31
Fish Soup (Catalonia) SP, 139
Fish Kebabs ME, 119
Flaming Pasta in Tomato Sauce IT,
73
Fondina IT, 70
Frascati IT, 72
Fresh Herb Omelette ME, 122
Fresh Pea Soup with Mint JE, 101
Fresh Smoked Fish with Curried
Pepper Sauce ME, 119
Fresh Red Chutney IN, 62
Fresh Sardines Baked in Vine
Leaves GR, 34
Fried Frogs Legs AC, 18
Fried Pork with Coriander ME, 124

G

Gallego Soup SP, 140
Garam Masala IN, 47
Gazpacho SP, 140
Ghee IN, 47
Gingerbread AC, 24
Ginger or Garlic Juice IN, 47
Gorgonzola IT, 70
Grecian Chicken with Onions GR, 38
Green Banana Curry IN, 59
Greek Creamed Rice GR, 40
Greek Gruyere GR, 42
Greek Honey Twists GR, 39
Greek Fried Mussels GR, 32

Greek Orange Compote GR, 40
Green Peppers Stuffed with Shrimps
IN, 56
Grilled Swordfish Steaks ME, 120,
Grilled Swordfish Steaks GR, 35
Guinea Fowl with Spicy Sauce IT, 83

H

Halibut with Wine and Cheese
Sauce JE, 103
Halva ME, 128
Herring Gundy AC, 18
Herring and Sour Cream Salad JE,
97
Honey Cakes JE, 108
Hot Peach Pickle IN, 63
Hunters Rabbit IT, 84

I

Iced Milk and Paw Paw Frappe AC,
26
Indian Chicken and Tomatoes IN, 52
Indian Fish Kebabs IN, 57
Indian Roasted Spiced Fish IN, 57
Italian Braised Beef IT, 84
Italian Brown Lentil Soup IT, 77
Italian Fruit Cake with Plum IT, 88
Italian Haricot Bean Soup IT, 77
Italian Herb Pancake IT, 74
Italian Scrambled Egg with Cheese
IT, 75
Italian Stuffed Peaches IT, 87

J

Jellied Orange Consome AC, 16

K

Kasseri GR, 42
Kheer Kamala IN, 64

L

Lamb Cooked in Paper GR, 37
Lambrusco IT, 72

NOTES

NOTES

SPECTRUM PUBLICATIONS

Spectrum Publications does not focus on books or publications confined by subject, category or classification. As its name implies, Spectrum publishes a wide range of interests whose common denominator is originality of thought or subject plus competence of content and its presentation. Such publications are few and difficult to find, but those that are found are worthy of as wide a dissemination as possible. To assist in the achievement of this objective promotions are primarily pursued on radio the ideal media for the fullest enjoyment of the images and excitement created by language. Pictures in the mind, whether created orally or aurally, are far superior to those seen on the screen.

Wherever it is appropriate, inter-action between author, publisher and reader is encouraged to their mutual benefit.

An example is the Spectrum Cook Book which will encourage participation in a unique competition designed to extend the interest and active involvement of its reader in the exploration and enjoyment of new tastes, new diets and new presentations. It could well be said that 'when a man tires of eating and drinking, he tires of living.'

SPECTRUM COOK BOOK INTERNATIONAL CUISINE COMPETITION

The purpose of this Competition is to widen the interest and therefore the enjoyment in the preparation, presentation and savouring of traditional cultural cuisines.

ENTRIES are invited for either or both of the following:

1. RECIPES that could have been included in any one or more of the seven sections in this book.

Awards will be made for originality of ingredients, simplicity of preparation, enjoyment of taste and uniqueness of presentation as a dish.

2. TABLE SETTINGS FOR SPECIFIC MEALS WHICH THEMSELVES INCORPORATE either a selection of various courses of differing cultural cuisines or a selection of courses drawn from one culture.

Awards will be made for originality and consistency of theme, combination of colour, dimension and tableware to create the desired atmosphere in which to enjoy the food and drink.

AWARDS will be:

1. Dinner for two at a leading cultural restaurant, the meal to include the winning recipe or table setting.

AND

2. Publication of the winning recipe in the second volume of the Spectrum Cook Book with appearance on local commercial radio.

The competition closes on August 31 1992. Entries can be sent direct to the commercial radio station promoting the competition or to the U.K. Distributors: Ashford Buchan & Enright, 31 Bridge Street, Leatherhead, Surrey KT22 8BN.